Statistical Physics

Tony Guénault is Reader in Physics at the University of Lancaster. His research career has centred around different aspects of low temperature physics, and for the last ten years (with George Pickett at Lancaster) he has been involved in attaining the lowest equilibrium temperatures anywhere in the world and in studying superfluid helium-3 at these temperatures.

STUDENT PHYSICS SERIES

Series Editor:
Professor R. J. Blin-Stoyle, FRS, *University of Sussex*
Advisory Editor:
Professor E. R. Dobbs, *University of London*

The aim of the *Student Physics Series* is to cover the material required for a first degree course in physics in a series of concise, clear and readable texts. Each volume will cover one of the usual sections of the physics degree course and will concentrate on covering the essential features of the subject. The texts will thus provide a core course in physics that all students should be expected to acquire, and to which more advanced work can be related according to ability. By concentrating on the essentials, the texts should also allow a valuable perspective and accessibility not normally attainable through the more usual textbooks. Select volumes at advanced undergraduate and first-year postgraduate level will also be included.

Already published:

Quantum Mechanics
  P. C. W. Davies
  'A very useful, readable and relatively inexpensive technical introduction to the subject.'—*THES*
Electricity and Magnetism
  E. R. Dobbs
  'Logically laid out, lucidly developed and well written...this clear account can be thoroughly recommended.'—*Physics Education*
Classical Mechanics
  B. P. Cowan
  'A very useful book, well worth a student's money.'—*Contemporary Physics*
Electromagnetic Waves
  E. R. Dobbs
  'Extremely clear...with fresh insights...can be thoroughly recommended.' —*Nature*
Liquids and Solids
  M. T. Sprackling
  'Remarkably clear and easy to follow.'—*THES*
Thermal Physics
  C. B. P. Finn
  'Will enrich the education of very large numbers of students for many years to come.' —*THES*
Elementary Particle Physics
  I. R. Kenyon
Relativity Physics
  R. E. Turner

STATISTICAL PHYSICS

A. M. GUÉNAULT

Reader in Physics
University of Lancaster

ROUTLEDGE
London and New York

First published in 1988 by Routledge
11 New Fetter Lane, London EC4P 4EE

Published in the USA by Routledge Inc.
in association with Methuen Inc.
29 West 35th Street, New York, NY 10001

Set in 10/12 Pt Times
by Thomson Press (India) Ltd, New Delhi
and printed in the British Isles
by the Guernsey Press Co Ltd
Guernsey Channel Islands

Library of Congress Cataloging in Publication Data
Guénault, A. M.
    Statistical physics by A. M. Guénault.
        p.   cm.   (Student physics series)
    Includes index.
    1. Statistical physics.   I. Title.   II. Series.
    QC174.8.G84 1988   87-19884
    530.1'3   dc 19

British Library CIP Data also available
ISBN 0-415-00259-1

CONTENTS

Preface   viii

Chapter 1 **Basic ideas**   1
1.1   The macrostate   1
1.2   Microstates   3
1.3   The averaging postulate   4
1.4   Distributions   6
1.5   The statistical method in outline   8
1.6   A model example   10
1.7   Statistical entropy and microstates   13

Chapter 2 **Distinguishable particles**   16
2.1   The thermal equilibrium distribution   17
2.2   What are α and β?   21
2.3   A statistical definition of temperature   22
2.4   The Boltzmann distribution and
        the partition function   26
2.5   Calculation of thermodynamic functions   27

Chapter 3 **Two examples**   30
3.1   A spin-$\frac{1}{2}$ solid   30
3.2   Localized harmonic oscillators   45

Chapter 4 **Gases: The density of states**   52
4.1   Fitting waves into boxes   53
4.2   Other information for statistical physics   57
4.3   An example – helium gas   60

Chapter 5 *Gases: The distributions*   62
5.1 Distribution in groups   62
5.2 Identical particles–fermions and bosons   64
5.3 Counting microstates for gases   67
5.4 The three distributions   72

Chapter 6 *Maxwell–Boltzmann gases*   76
6.1 The validity of the Maxwell–Boltzmann limit   76
6.2 The Maxwell–Boltzmann distribution of
        speeds   79
6.3 The connection to thermodynamics   82

Chapter 7 *Diatomic gases*   87
7.1 Energy contributions in diatomic gases   87
7.2 Heat capacity of a diatomic gas   89
7.3 The heat capacity of hydrogen   93

Chapter 8 *Fermi–Dirac gases*   99
8.1 Properties of an ideal Fermi–Dirac gas   100
8.2 Application to metals   109
8.3 Application to helium-3   111

Chapter 9 *Bose–Einstein Gases*   115
9.1 Properties of an ideal Bose–Einstein gas   115
9.2 Application to helium-4   121
9.3 Phoney bosons   124

Chapter 10 *Entropy in other situations*   132
10.1 Entropy and disorder   132
10.2 An assembly at fixed temperature   135
10.3 Vacancies in solids   138

Chapter 11 *Phase transitions*   141
11.1 Types of phase transition   141
11.2 Ferromagnetism of a spin-$\frac{1}{2}$ solid   143
11.3 Real ferromagnetic materials   150
11.4 Order–disorder transformations in alloys   152

Chapter 12 *Two new ideas*   155
12.1   Statics or dynamics?   155
12.2   Ensembles–a larger view   159

Appendix 1 *Some elementary counting problems*   166
Appendix 2 *Some problems with large numbers*   168
Appendix 3 *Some useful integrals*   171
Appendix 4 *Some useful constants*   174
Appendix 5 *Questions*   175
Appendix 6 *Answers to questions*   182

Index   184

PREFACE

Statistical physics is not a difficult subject, and I trust that this will not be found a difficult book. It contains much that a number of generations of Lancaster students have studied with me, as part of their physics honours degree work. The lecture course was of twenty hours duration, and I have added comparatively little to the lecture syllabus. A prerequisite is that the reader should have a working knowledge of basic thermal physics (i.e. the laws of thermodynamics and their application to simple substances). The book *Thermal Physics* by Colin Finn in this series forms an ideal introduction.

Statistical physics has a thousand and one different ways of approaching the same basic results. I have chosen a rather down-to-earth and unsophisticated approach, without I hope totally obscuring the considerable interest of the fundamentals. This enables applications to be introduced at an early stage in the book.

As a low-temperature physicist, I have always found a particular interest in statistical physics, and especially in how the absolute zero is approached. I should not, therefore, apologize for the low-temperature bias in the topics which I have selected from the many possibilities.

Without burdening them with any responsibility for my competence, I would like to acknowledge how much I have learned in very different ways from my first three 'bosses' as a trainee physicist: Brian Pippard, Keith MacDonald and Sydney Dugdale. More recently my colleagues at Lancaster, George Pickett, David Meredith, Peter McClintock, Arthur Clegg and many others have done much to keep me on the rails. Finally, but most of all, I should thank my wife Joan for her encouragement.

A PLAIN MAN'S GUIDE TO STATISTICAL PHYSICS

Chapter 1
Basic ideas

There is an obvious problem about getting to grips with an understanding of matter in thermal equilibrium. Let us suppose you are interested (as a designer of saucepans?) in the thermal capacity of copper at 450 K. On the one hand you can turn to thermodynamics, but this approach is of such generality that it is often difficult to see the point. Relationships between the principal heat capacities, the thermal expansion coefficient and the compressibility are all very well, but they do not help you to understand the particular magnitude and temperature dependence of the actual heat capacity of copper. On the other hand, you can see that what is needed is a microscopic mechanical picture of what is going on inside the copper. However, this picture becomes impossibly detailed when one starts to discuss the laws of motion of 10^{24} or so copper atoms.

The aim of statistical physics is to make a bridge between the over-elaborate detail of mechanics and the obscure generalities of thermodynamics. In this chapter we shall look at one way of making such a bridge. Most readers will already be familiar with the kinetic theory of ideal gases. The treatment given here will enable us to discuss a much wider variety of matter than this, although there will nevertheless be some limitations to the traffic that can travel across the bridge.

1.1 The macrostate

The basic task of statistical physics is to take a system which is in a well-defined thermodynamic state and to compute the various thermodynamic properties of that system from an (assumed) microscopic model.

The '*macrostate*' is another word for the thermodynamic state of the system. It is a specification of a system which contains just enough information for its thermodynamic state to be well defined, but no more information than that. As outlined in most books on thermal physics (e.g. Finn's book *Thermal Physics* in this series), for the simple case of a pure substance this will involve:

the nature of the substance–e.g. natural copper

the amount of the substance–e.g. 1.5 moles

a small number of pairs of thermodynamic co-ordinates–e.g. pressure P and volume V; magnetic field B and magnetization M; surface tension and surface area, etc.

Each of these pairs is associated with a way of doing work on the system. For many systems only $P-V$ work is relevant, and (merely for brevity) we shall phrase what follows in terms of $P-V$ work only. Magnetic systems will also appear later in the book.

In practice the two co-ordinates specified, rather than being P and V, will be those appropriate to the external conditions. For instance, the lump of copper might be at a specific pressure P ($= 1$ atm) and temperature T ($= 450$ K). In this case the macrostate would be defined by P and T; and the volume V and internal energy U and other parameters would then all be determined in principle from P and T. It is precisely one of the objectives of statistical physics to obtain from first principles what are these values of V, U, etc. (In fact, we need not set our sights as low as this. Statistical physics also gives detailed insights into dynamical properties, and an example of this is given in Chapter 12.)

Now comes, by choice, an important limitation. In order to have a concrete situation to discuss in this chapter (and indeed throughout the first eight chapters of this book), we shall concentrate on one particular type of macrostate, *namely that appropriate to an isolated system.* Therefore the macrostate will be defined by: the nature of the substance, the amount, and by U and V. For the isolated system in its energy-proof enclosure, the internal energy is a fixed constant, and V is also constant since no work is to be done on the system. The (fixed) amount of the substance we can characterize by the number N of microscopic 'particles' making up the system.

This limitation is not too severe in practice. For an isolated system in which N is reasonably large, fluctuations in (say) T are small and one finds that T is determined really rather precisely by (N, U, V). Consequently one can use results based on the (N, U, V) macrostate in order to discuss equally well the behaviour in any other macrostate, such as the (N, P, T) macrostate appropriate to our piece of copper.

1.2 Microstates

Let us now consider the mechanical microscopic properties of the system of interest, which we are assuming to be an assembly of N identical microscopic particles. For the given (N, U, V) macrostate there are an enormous number of possible '*microstates*'.

The word microstate means the most detailed specification of the assembly that can be imagined. For example, in the classical kinetic theory of gases, the microstate would need to specify the (vector) position and momentum of each of the N gas particles, a total of $6N$ co-ordinates. (Actually even this is assuming that each particle is a structureless point, with no internal degrees of freedom like rotation, vibration, etc.) Of course, this microstate contains a totally indigestible amount of information, far too much for one to store even one microstate in the largest available computer. But, worse still, the system changes its microstate very rapidly indeed—for instance one mole of a typical gas will change its microstate roughly 10^{32} times a second.

Clearly some sort of averaging over microstates is needed. And here is one of those happy occasions where quantum mechanics turns out to be a lot easier than classical mechanics.

The conceptual problem for classical microstates, as outlined above for a gas, is that they are infinite in number. The triumph of Boltzmann—had he lived to see the full justification of it—and of Gibbs around the turn of the century, was to see how to do the averaging nevertheless. They observed that a system spends equal times in equal volumes of 'phase-space' (a combined position and momentum space; see e.g. Finn's *Thermal Physics*, Chapter 5). Hence the volume in phase-space can be used as a statistical weight for microstates within that volume. Splitting the whole of phase-space into small volume elements, therefore, leads to a feasible procedure for averaging over all microstates as required. However, we can nowadays adopt a much simpler approach.

In quantum mechanics a microstate by definition is *a quantum state of the whole assembly*. It can be described by a single N-particle wave function, containing all the information possible about the state of the system. The point to appreciate is that quantum states are discrete in principle. Hence although the macrostate (N, U, V) has an enormous number of possible microstates consistent with it, the number is none the less definite and finite. We shall call this number Ω, and it turns out to play a central role in the statistical treatment.

1.3 The averaging postulate

We now come to the assumption which is the whole basis of statistical physics:

All accessible microstates are equally probable.

This averaging postulate is to be treated as an assumption, but it is of interest to observe that it is nevertheless a reasonable one. Two types of supporting argument can be produced.

The first argument is to talk about time-averages. Making any physical measurement (say, of the pressure of a gas on the wall of its container) takes a non-zero time; and in the time of the measurement the system will have passed through a *very* large number of microstates. In fact this is why we get a reproducible value of P; observable fluctuations are small over the appropriate time scale. Hence it is reasonable that we should be averaging effectively over all accessible microstates. The qualification 'accessible' is included to allow for the possibility of metastability. There can be situations in which groups of microstates are not in fact accessed in the time scale of the measurement, so that there is in effect another constant of the motion, besides N, U and V; only a subset of the total number Ω of microstates should then be averaged. We shall return to this point in later chapters, but will assume for the present that all Ω microstates are readily accessible from each other. Hence the time-average argument indicates that averaging over all microstates is necessary. The necessity to average *equally* over all of them is not so obvious, rather it is assumed. (In passing one can note that for a gas this point relates to the even coverage of classical phase-space as mentioned above, in that quantum states are evenly dispersed through phase-space; for example see Chapter 4.)

The second type of supporting argument is to treat the postulate as a 'confession of ignorance', a common stratagem in quantum mechanics. Since we do not in fact know which one of the Ω microstates the system is in at the time of interest, we simply average equally over all possibilities, i.e. over all microstates. This is often called an 'ensemble' average, in that one can visualize it as replicating the measurement in a whole set of identical systems and then averaging over the whole set (or ensemble).

One can note that the equality of ensemble and time averages implies a particular kind of uniformity in a thermodynamic system. To give an allied social example, consider the insurer's problem. He wishes to charge a fair (sic) premium for life insurance. Thus he requires an expectation of life for those currently alive, but he cannot get this by following them with a stop-watch until they die.

Rather, he can look at biographical records in the mortuary in order to determine an expectation of life (for the wrong sample) and hope for uniformity.

1.4 Distributions

In attempting to average over all Ω microstates we still have a formidable problem. A typical system (e.g. a mole of gas) is an assembly of $N = 10^{24}$ particles. That is a large enough number, but the number Ω of microstates is of order N^N, an astronomically large number. We must confess that knowledge of the system at the microstate level is too detailed for us to handle, and therefore we should restrict our curiosity merely to a *distribution* specification, defined below.

A distribution involves assigning individual (private) energies to each of the N particles. This is only sensible (or indeed possible) for an assembly of *weakly interacting particles*. The reason is that we shall wish to express the total internal energy U of the assembly as the sum of the individual energies of the N particles:

$$U = \sum_{l=1}^{N} \varepsilon(l) \tag{1.1}$$

where $\varepsilon(l)$ is the energy of the lth particle. Any such expression implies that the interaction energies between particles are much smaller than these (self) energies ε. Actually any thermodynamic system must have some interaction between its particles, otherwise it would never reach equilibrium. The requirement rather is for the interaction to be small enough for equation (1.1) to be valid, hence 'weakly interacting' rather than 'non-interacting' particles.

Of course this restriction of approach is extremely limiting, although less so than one might first suspect. Clearly, since the restriction is also one of the assumptions of simple kinetic theory, our treatment will be useful for perfect gases. However, it means that for a real fluid having strong interactions between molecules, i.e. an imperfect gas or a liquid, the method cannot be applied. We shall return briefly to this point in Chapter 13, but a full treatment of interacting particles is well outside the scope of this book. At first sight it might seem that a description of solids is also outside this framework, since interactions between atoms are obviously strong in a solid. However, we shall see that many of the thermal properties of solids are nevertheless to be understood from a model based on an assembly of N weakly interacting particles, when one recognizes that these particles need not be the atoms, but other appropriate entities. For example the particles can be phonons for a discussion of lattice vibrations (Chapter 9); localized spins for a discussion of magnetic properties (Chapter 2 and 11); or conduction electrons for a description of metals and semiconductors (Chapter 8).

A *distribution* then relates to the energies of a single particle. For each microstate of the assembly of N identical weakly interacting particles, each particle is in an identifiable one-particle state. In the distribution specification, intermediate in detail between the macrostate and a microstate, we choose not to investigate *which* particles are in which states, but only to specify the total *number* of particles in the states.

We shall use two alternative definitions of a distribution.

Definition 1 – Distribution in states

This is a set of numbers $(n_1, n_2, \ldots, n_j, \ldots)$ where the typical distribution number n_j is defined as the number of particles in state j, which has energy ε_j. Often, but not always, this distribution will be an infinite set; the label j must run over all the possible states for one particle. A useful shorthand for the whole set of distribution numbers $(n_1, n_2, \ldots, n_j, \ldots)$ is simply $\{n_j\}$.

The above definition is the one we shall adopt until we specifically discuss gases (Chapter 4 onwards), at which stage an alternative, and somewhat less detailed, definition becomes useful.

Definition 2 – Distribution in levels

This is a set of numbers $(n_1, n_2, \ldots, n_i, \ldots)$ for which the typical number n_i is now defined as the number of particles in level i, which has energy ε_i and degeneracy g_i, the degeneracy being defined as the number of states belonging to that level. The shorthand $\{n_i\}$ will be adopted for this distribution.

It is worth pointing out that the definition to be adopted is a matter of one's choice. The first definition is the more detailed, and is perfectly capable of handling the case of degenerate levels – degeneracy simply means that not all the ε_js are different. We shall reserve the label j for the states description and the label i for the levels description; it is arguable that the n symbols should also be differentiated, but we shall not do this.

Specifications – an example

Before proceeding with physics, an all too familiar example helps to clarify the difference between the three types of specification of a system, the macrostate, the distribution, and the microstate.

The example concerns the marks of a class of students. The macrostate specification is that the class of 51 students had an average mark of 55 per cent. (No detail at all, but that's thermodynamics.) The microstate is quite unambiguous and clear; it will specify the name of each of the 51 individuals and his/her mark. (Full detail, nowhere to hide!) The definition of the distribution, as above, is to some extent a matter of choice. But a typical distribution would give the number of students achieving marks in each decade, a total of 10 distribution numbers. (Again all identity of individuals is lost, but more statistical detail is retained than in the macrostate.)

1.5 The statistical method in outline

The object of the exercise is now to use the fundamental averaging assumption about microstates (section 1.3) to discover the particular distribution $\{n_j\}$ (section 1.4) which best describes the thermal equilibrium properties of the system.

We are considering an isolated system consisting of a fixed number N of the identical weakly interacting particles contained in a fixed volume V and with a fixed internal energy U. There are essentially four steps towards the statistical description of this macrostate which we discuss in turn:

   I. Solve the one-particle problem.
  II. Enumerate possible distributions.
 III. Count the microstates corresponding to each distribution.
 IV. Find the average distribution.

1.5.1 The one-particle problem

This is a purely mechanical problem, and since it involves only one particle it is a soluble problem for many cases of interest. The solution gives the states of a particle which we label by j ($= 0$, 1, 2,...). The corresponding energies are ε_j. We should note that these energies depend on V (for a gas) or on V/N the volume per particle (for a solid).

1.5.2 Possible distributions

The possible sets of distribution numbers $\{n_j\}$ can now be simply written down (given appropriate patience, because usually there will be very many possibilities). However, we give this relatively straightforward task a section of its own, in order to stress that a valid distribution must satisfy the two conditions implied by the macrostate:

$$\sum_j n_j = N \tag{1.2}$$

$$\sum_j n_j \varepsilon_j = U. \tag{1.3}$$

Equation (1.2) ensures that the distribution contains the correct number of particles. Equation (1.3) follows from (1.1), and guarantees that distribution corresponds to the correct value of U. All of the conditions of the (N, U, V) macrostate are now taken care of.

1.5.3 Counting microstates

Next we need to count up the number of microstates consistent with each valid set of distribution numbers. Usually, and especially for a large system, each distribution $\{n_j\}$ will be associated with a very large number of microstates. This number we call $t(\{n_j\})$. The dependence of t on $\{n_j\}$ is a pure combinatorial problem. The result is very different for an assembly of localized particles (in which the particles are distinguishable by their locality) and for an assembly of gas-like particles (in which the particles are fundamentally indistinguishable). Hence the statistical details for localized particles and for gases are treated below in separate chapters.

1.5.4 The average distribution

The reason for counting microstates is that, according to the postulate of equal probability of all microstates, the number $t(\{n_j\})$ is the *statistical weight* of the distribution $\{n_j\}$. Hence we can now in principle make the correct weighted average over all possible distributions to determine the average distribution $\{n_j\}_{av}$. And this average distribution, according to our postulates, is the one which describes the thermal equilibrium distribution.

1.6 A model example

Before further discussion of the properties of a large system, the realistic case in thermodynamics, let us investigate the properties of a small model system using the methodology of the previous section.

1.6.1 A simple assembly

The macrostate we consider is an assembly of $N = 4$ distinguishable particles. We label the four particles A, B, C and D. The total energy $U = 4\varepsilon$, where ε is a constant (whose value depends on V).

Step I. The mechanical problem is to be solved to give the possible states of one particle. We take the solution to be states of (non-degenerate) energies 0, ε, 2ε, 3ε,.... For convenience we label these states $j = 0, 1, 2, \ldots$ with $\varepsilon_j = j\varepsilon$.

Step II. Defining the distribution numbers as $\{n_j\}$, with $j = 0, 1, 2, \ldots$, we note that any allowable distributions must satisfy:

$$\Sigma n_j = 4; \qquad \Sigma n_j \varepsilon_j = 4\varepsilon \quad \text{(i.e. } \Sigma n_j j = 4\text{)}.$$

There are thus five possible distributions:

Distribution	n_0	n_1	n_2	n_3	n_4	n_5	...
1	3	0	0	0	1	0	...
2	2	1	0	1	0	0	...
3	2	0	2	0	0	0	...
4	1	2	1	0	0	0	...
5	0	4	0	0	0	0	...

Step III. A microstate specifies the state of each of the four particles. We need to count the number of microstates to each of the five distributions. To take distribution 1 as an example, we can identify four possible microstates:

  (i) A is in state $j = 4$; B, C and D are in state $j = 0$
  (ii) B is in state $j = 4$, the others are in state $j = 0$
 (iii) C is in state $j = 4$, the others are in state $j = 0$
 (iv) D is in state $j = 4$, the others are in state $j = 0$

Hence $t^{(1)} = 4$. Similarly one can work out (an exercise for the reader?) the numbers of microstates for the other four distributions. The answers are $t^{(2)} = 12$, $t^{(3)} = 6$, $t^{(4)} = 12$, $t^{(5)} = 1$. It is significant that the distributions which spread the particles between the states as much as possible have the most microstates, and thus (Step IV) are the most probable. The total number of microstates Ω is equal to the sum $t^{(1)} + t^{(2)} + t^{(3)} + t^{(4)} + t^{(5)}$, i.e. $\Omega = 35$ in this example.

(*Aside.* A general formula for this situation is developed in Appendix 1 and we shall make much use of it in Chapter 2.

The result is:

$$t(\{n_j\}) = N!/\prod_j n_j! \tag{1.4}$$

where the denominator $\prod n_j!$ represents the extended product $n_0! n_1! n_2! \ldots n_j! \ldots$. The result for $t^{(1)}$ follows from equation (1.4) as $4!/3!$, when one substitutes $0! = 1$ and $1! = 1$. The other t values follow similarly.)

Step IV. The average value of every distribution number can now be obtained by an equal averaging over every microstate, readily computed as a weighted mean over the five possible distributions using the t values as the weight. For instance:

$$\begin{aligned}(n_0)_{av} &= (n_0^{(1)} t^{(1)} + n_0^{(2)} t^{(2)} + \ldots)/\Omega \\ &= (3 \times 4 + 2 \times 12 + 2 \times 6 + 1 \times 12 + 0 \times 1)/35 \\ &= 60/35 = 1.71.\end{aligned}$$

Similarly for n_1, n_2 etc. give finally:

$$\{n_j\}_{av} = (1.71, 1.14, 0.69, 0.34, 0.11, 0, 0 \ldots).$$

The result is not unlike a falling exponential curve, the general result for a large assembly which we shall derive in the next chapter.

1.6.2 A composite assembly

We now briefly reconsider the four-particle model assembly as a composite two-part assembly. We take as an initial macrostate a more restrictive situation than before. Let us suppose that the two particles A and B form one sub-assembly, which is thermally isolated from a second sub-assembly consisting of particles C and D. The values of internal energies are $U_{AB} = 4\varepsilon$, $U_{CD} = 0$. This initial macrostate is more fully specified than the situation in section 1.6.1, since the division of energy between AB and CD is fixed.

The total number of microstates is now only five rather than 35. This arises as follows. For sub-assembly CD we must have $j = 0$ for both particles, the only way to achieve $U_{CD} = 0$. Hence $\Omega_{CD} = 1$ and $\{n_j\} = (2,0,0,0,\ldots)$. (This result corresponds to a low-temperature distribution, as we shall see later, in that all the particles are in the lowest state). For sub-assembly AB there are five microstates to give $U_{AB} = 4\varepsilon$. In a notation $[j(A), j(B)]$ they are $[4,0]$, $[0,4]$, $[3,1]$, $[1,3]$, $[2,2]$. Hence $\Omega_{AB} = 5$ and $\{n_j\} = (0.4, 0.4, 0.4, 0.4, 0.4, 0, 0, \ldots)$. (This is now a high temperature distribution, with the states becoming more evenly populated.)

In order to find the total number of microstates of any composite two-part assembly, the values of Ω for the two sub-assemblies must be multiplied together. This is because for every microstate of the one sub-assembly, the other sub-assembly can be in any one of its microstates. Therefore in this case we have $\Omega = \Omega_{AB}.\Omega_{CD} = 5$, as stated earlier.

Now let us place the two sub-assemblies in thermal contact with each other, while still remaining isolated from the rest of the universe. This removes the restriction of the $4:0$ energy division between AB and CD, and the macrostate reverts to exactly the same as in section 1.6.1. When equilibrium is reached, this then implies a distribution intermediate in shape (temperature) as derived above. But of particular importance is the new value of Ω (namely 35). One way of understanding the great increase (and indeed another way of calculating it) is to appreciate that microstates with $U_{AB} = 3\varepsilon, 2\varepsilon, \varepsilon, 0$ are now accessible in addition to 4ε; and correspondingly for U_{CD}. So we can observe from this example that internal adjustments of an isolated system towards overall equilibrium *increase* the number of accessible microstates.

1.7 Statistical entropy and microstates

First, a word about entropy. Entropy is introduced in thermodynamics as that rather shadowy function of the state of a system associated with the second law of thermodynamics. The essence of the idea concerns the direction (the 'arrow of time') of spontaneous or natural processes, i.e. processes which are found to occur in practice.

A pretty example is the mixing of sugar and sand. Start with a dish containing a discrete pile of each substance. The sugar and sand may then be mixed by stirring, but the inverse process of reseparating the substances by unstirring (stirring in the opposite direction?) does not in practice happen. Unmixing can only be achieved with great ingenuity. In a natural process, the second law tells us that the entropy S of the universe (or of any isolated system) never decreases. And in the mixing process the entropy increases. (The 'great ingenuity' would involve a larger increase of entropy somewhere else in the universe). All this is a statement of probability, rather than of necessity—it is *possible* in principle to separate the mixed sugar and sand by stirring, but it is almost infinitely *improbable*. And thermodynamics is the science of the probable!

Statistical physics enables one to discuss entropy in terms of probability in a direct and simple way. We shall adopt in this book a statistical definition for the entropy of an isolated system:

$$S = k_B \ln \Omega \qquad (1.5)$$

with k_B equal to Boltzmann's constant $1.38 \times 10^{-23} \text{ J K}^{-1}$. This definition has an old history, originating from Boltzmann's work on the kinetic theory of gases in the last century, and equation (1.5) appears on Boltzmann's tombstone. The relationship was developed further by Planck in his studies of heat radiation—the start of the quantum theory.

Logically perhaps equation (1.5) is a derived *result* of statistical physics. However, it is such a central ideal that it is sensible to introduce it at this stage, and to treat it as a *definition* of entropy from the outset. We shall gradually see that the S so defined has all the properties of the usual thermodynamic entropy.

What we have observed so far about the behaviour of Ω is certainly consistent with equation (1.5).

1. As noted above, for an isolated system a natural process, i.e. one which spontaneously occurs as the system attains overall equilibrium, is precisely one in which the thermodynamic entropy increases. And we have seen in the example of section 1.6 that Ω also increases in this type of process. Hence a direct relation between S and Ω is suggested, and moreover a monotonically increasing one in agreement with equation (1.5).

2. For a composite assembly, made up of two sub-assemblies 1 and 2 say, we have shown in section 1.6.2 that the number of microstates of the whole assembly Ω is given by $\Omega = \Omega_1 . \Omega_2$. The required behaviour of the thermodynamic entropy is of course $S = S_1 + S_2$, and the relation (1.5) is consistent with this; indeed the logarithm is the only function which will give the result. (This was Planck's original 'proof' of equation (1.5).)

3. The correlation between entropy and the number of microstates accessible (i.e. essentially a measure of disorder) is a very appealing one. It interprets the third law of thermodynamics to suggest that all matter which comes to equilibrium will *order* at the absolute zero in the sense that only one microstate will be accessed ($\Omega = 1$ corresponding to $S = 0$, a natural zero for entropy).

Later in the book, we shall see much more evidence in favour of equation (1.5), the final test being that the results derived using it are correct, for example the equation of state of an ideal gas (Chapter 6), and the relation of entropy to temperature and heat (Chapter 2).

Chapter 2
Distinguishable particles

The next step is to apply the statistical method outlined in Chapter 1 to realistic thermodynamic systems. This means addressing the properties of an assembly which consists of a large number N of weakly interacting identical particles. There are two types of assembly which fulfil the requirements.

One type is a gaseous assembly, in which the identical particles are the gas molecules themselves. In quantum mechanics one recognizes that the molecules are not only identical, but they are also (in principle as well as in practice) indistinguishable. It is not possible to 'put a blob of red paint' on one particular molecule and to follow its history. Hence the microstate description must take full account of the indistinguishability of the particles. Gaseous assemblies will be introduced later in Chapter 4.

In this chapter we shall treat the other type of assembly, in which the particles are distinguishable. The physical example is that of a solid rather than that of a gas. Consider a simple solid which is made up of N identical atoms. It remains true that the atoms themselves are indistinguishable. However, a good description of our assembly is to think about the solid as a set of N lattice sites, in which each lattice site contains an atom. A 'particle' of the assembly then becomes 'the atom at lattice site 4357 (or whatever)'. (*Which* of the atoms is at this site is not specified.) The particle is distinguished not by the identity of the atom, but by the distinct location of each lattice site. A solid is an assembly of localized particles, and it is this locality which makes the particles distinguishable.

We shall now develop the statistical description of an ideal solid, in which the atoms are weakly interacting. How far the behaviour of real solids can be explained in this way will become clearer in later chapters. The main results of this chapter will be the derivation of the thermal equilibrium distribution (the Boltzmann distribution) together with methods for the calculation of thermodynamic quantities. Two physical examples are given in Chapter 3.

2.1 The thermal equilibrium distribution

We follow the method outlined in section 1.5. For the macrostate we consider an assembly of N identical distinguishable (localized) particles contained in a fixed volume V and having a fixed internal energy U. The system is mechanically and thermally isolated, but we shall be considering sufficiently large assemblies that the other thermodynamic quantities (T, S, etc.) are well defined.

2.1.1 The one-particle states

The one-particle states will be specified by a state label j ($= 0, 1, 2 \ldots$). The corresponding energies ε_j may or may not be all different. These states will be dependent upon the volume per particle (V/N) for our localized assembly.

2.1.2 Possible distributions

We use the distribution in states $\{n_j\}$ defined in section 1.4. The distribution numbers must satisfy the two conditions (1.2) and (1.3) imposed by the macrostate:

$$\sum_j n_j = N \qquad \text{(1.2) and (2.1)}$$

$$\sum_j n_j \varepsilon_j = U. \qquad \text{(1.3) and (2.2)}$$

2.1.3 Counting microstates

It is here that the fact that we have distinguishable particles shows up. It means that the particles can be counted just as macroscopic objects. A microstate will specify the state (i.e.

the label j) for each distinct particle. We wish to count up how many such microstates there are to an allowable distribution $\{n_j\}$. The problem is essentially the same as that discussed in Appendix 1, namely the possible arrangements of N objects into piles with n_j in a typical pile. The answer is:

$$t(\{n_j\}) = N!/\prod_j n_j!. \qquad (1.4) \text{ and } (2.3)$$

2.1.4 The average distribution

According to our postulate, the thermal distribution should now be obtained by evaluating the average distribution $\{n_j\}_{av}$. This task involves a weighted average of all the possible distributions (as allowed by equations (2.1) and (2.2)) using the values of t (equation (2.3)) as statistical weights. This task can be performed, but fortunately we are saved from the necessity of having to do anything so complicated by the large numbers involved. Some of the simplifications of large numbers are explored briefly in Appendix 2.

The vital point is that it turns out that one distribution, say $\{n_j^*\}$, is overwhelmingly more probable than any of the others. In other words, the function $t(\{n_j\})$ is very sharply peaked indeed around $\{n_j^*\}$. Hence, rather than averaging over all possible distributions, one can obtain essentially the same result by picking out the most probable distribution alone. This then reduces to the mathematical problem of maximizing $t(\{n_j\})$ from equation (2.3) subject to the conditions (2.1) and (2.2).

Another even stronger way of looking at the sharp peaking of t is to consider the relationship between Ω and t. Since Ω is defined as the total number of microstates contained by the macrostate, it follows that:

$$\Omega = \sum t(\{n_j\})$$

where the sum goes over all distributions. What is now suggested (and compare the pennies problem of Appendix 2) is that this sum can in practice be replaced by its maximum term, i.e.:

$$\Omega \approx t(\{n_j^*\}) = t^* \text{ (for short)}. \tag{2.4}$$

2.1.5 The most probable distribution

To find the thermal equilibrium distribution, we need to find the maximum t^* and to identify the distribution $\{n_j^*\}$ at this maximum. Actually it is a lot simpler to work with $\ln t$, rather than t itself. Since $\ln x$ is a monotonically increasing function of x, this does not change the problem; it just makes the solution a lot more straightforward. Taking logarithms of (2.3) we obtain:

$$\ln t = \ln N! - \sum_j \ln n_j!. \tag{2.5}$$

Here the large numbers come to our aid. Assuming that all the ns are large enough for Stirling's approximation (Appendix 2) to be used, we can eliminate the factorials to obtain:

$$\ln t = (N \ln N - N) - \sum_j (n_j \ln n_j - n_j). \tag{2.6}$$

To find the maximum value of $\ln t$ from (2.6) we express changes in the distribution numbers as differentials (large numbers again!) so that the maximum will be obtained by differentiating $\ln t$ and setting the result equal to zero. Using the fact that N is constant, and noting the cancellation of two out of the three terms arising from the sum in (2.6), this gives simply:

$$d(\ln t) = 0 - \sum_j dn_j (\ln n_j + n_j/n_j - 1)$$
$$= - \sum_j \ln n_j^* \, dn_j = 0 \tag{2.7}$$

where the dn_js represent any allowable changes in the distribution numbers from the required distribution $\{n_j^*\}$. Of course not all changes are allowed. Only changes which maintain the correct values of N (2.1) and of U (2.2) may be countenanced. This lack of independence of the dn_js gives two restrictive conditions, obtained by differentiating (2.1) and (2.2):

$$d(N) = \sum_j dn_j = 0 \tag{2.8}$$

$$d(U) = \sum_j \varepsilon_j \, dn_j = 0. \tag{2.9}$$

A convenient way of dealing with the mathematics of a restricted maximum of this type is to use the Lagrange method of undetermined multipliers. The argument in our case goes as follows. First we note that we can self-evidently add any arbitrary multiples of equations (2.8) and (2.9) to equation (2.7), and still achieve the result zero. Thus:

$$\sum_j (-\ln n_j^* + \alpha + \beta \varepsilon_j) \, dn_j = 0 \tag{2.10}$$

for *any* values of the constants α and β. The second and clever step is then to recognize that it will always be possible to write the solution in such a way that each individual term in the sum of equation (2.10) equals zero, so long as specific values of α and β are chosen. In other words the most probable distribution $\{n_j^*\}$ will be given by:

$$(-\ln n_j^* + \alpha + \beta \varepsilon_j) = 0 \tag{2.11}$$

with α and β each having a specific (but as yet undetermined) value. This equation can then be written:

$$n_j^* = \exp(\alpha + \beta \varepsilon_j) \tag{2.12}$$

and this is the *Boltzmann Distribution*. We may note at once that it has the exponential form suggested for the thermal equilibrium distribution by the little example in Chapter 1. But before we can appreciate the significance of this central result, we need to explore the meanings of these constants α and β. (*A note of caution*: α and β are defined with the opposite sign in some other works. Looking at a familiar result (e.g. the Boltzmann distribution) easily makes this ambiguity clear.)

2.2 What are α and β?

Here (as ever?) physics and mathematics go hand in hand. In the mathematics, α was introduced as a multiplier for the number condition (2.1), and β for the energy condition (2.2). So it will follow that α is determined from the fixed number N of particles, and can be thought of as a 'potential for particle number'. Similarly β is determined by ensuring that the distribution describes an assembly with the correct energy U, and it can be interpreted as a 'potential for energy'.

2.2.1 α and number

Since α enters the Boltzmann distribution in such a simple way, this section will be short! We determine α by applying the condition (2.1) which caused its introduction in the first place. Substituting (2.12) back into (2.1) we obtain:

$$N = \sum_j n_j = \exp(\alpha) \sum_j (\beta \varepsilon_j) \tag{2.13}$$

since $\exp(\alpha)$ $(= A$, say$)$ is a factor in each term of the distribution. In other words, A is a normalization constant for the distribution, chosen so that the distribution describes the thermal properties of the correct number N of particles. Another way of writing (2.13) is: $A = N/Z$, with the 'partition function', Z, defined by $Z = \sum \exp(\beta \varepsilon_j)$. We may then write the Boltzmann distribution (2.12) as:

$$n_j = A \exp(\beta \varepsilon_j) = (N/Z) \exp(\beta \varepsilon_j). \tag{2.14}$$

We leave any fuller discussion of the partition function until later in the chapter, when the nature of β has been clarified.

2.2.2 β and energy

In contrast, the way in which β enters the Boltzmann distribution is more subtle. Nevertheless the formal statements are easily made. We substitute the thermal distribution (2.14) back into the relevant condition (2.2) to obtain:

$$U = \sum_j n_j \varepsilon_j = (N/Z) \sum_j \varepsilon_j \exp(\beta \varepsilon_j)$$

or $\quad U/N = \sum_j \varepsilon_j \exp(\beta\varepsilon_j)/\sum_j \exp(\beta\varepsilon_j).$ $\qquad$ (2.15)

The appropriate value of β is then that one which, when put into this equation, gives precisely the internal energy per particle (U/N) specified by the macrostate. Unfortunately this is not a very tidy result, but it is as far as we can go explicitly, since one cannot in general invert equation (2.15) to give an explicit formula for β as a function of (U, V, N). Nevertheless for a given (U, V, N) macrostate, β is fully specified by equation (2.15), and one can indeed describe it as a 'potential for energy', in that the equation gives a very direct correlation between (U/N) and β.

However, that is not the end of the story. It turns out that this untidy (but absolutely specific) function β has a very clear physical meaning in terms of thermodynamic functions other than (U, V, N). In fact we shall see that it must be related to *temperature* only, a sufficiently important point that the following section will be devoted to it.

2.3 A statistical definition of temperature

2.3.1 β and temperature

To show that there is a necessary relationship between β and temperature T, we consider the thermodynamic and statistical treatments of two systems in thermal equilibrium.

The thermodynamic treatment is obvious. Two systems in thermal equilibrium have, effectively by definition, the same temperature. This statement is based on the 'zeroth law of thermodynamics', which states that there is some common function of state shared by all systems in mutual thermal equilibrium – and this function of state is what is meant by (empiric) temperature.

The statistical treatment can follow directly the lines of section 2.1. The problem can be set up as follows. Consider two systems P and Q which are in thermal contact with each other, but together are isolated from the rest of the universe. The statistical method applies to this composite assembly in much the same way as in the simple example of section 1.6.2.

We suppose that system P consists of a fixed number N_P of localized particles, which each have states of energy ε_j, as before. The system Q need not be of the same type, so we take it as containing N_Q particles whose energy states are ε_k'. The corresponding distributions are $\{n_j\}$ for system P and $\{n_k'\}$ for system Q. Clearly the restrictions on the distributions are:

$$\sum_j n_j = N_P \tag{2.16}$$

$$\sum_k n_k' = N_Q \tag{2.17}$$

and $$\sum_j n_j \varepsilon_j + \sum_k n_k' \varepsilon_k' = U \tag{2.18}$$

where U is the total energy (i.e. $U_P + U_Q$) of the two systems together.

The counting of microstates is easy when we recall (section 1.6.2) that we may write:

$$\Omega = \Omega_P \times \Omega_Q \qquad \text{or} \qquad t = t_P \times t_Q \tag{2.19}$$

with the expressions for t_P and t_Q being analogous to equation (2.3).

Finding the most probable distribution may again be achieved by the Lagrange method as in section 2.1.5. The problem is to maximize $\ln t$ with t as given in equation (2.19), subject now to the three conditions (2.16), (2.17) and (2.18). Using multipliers α_P, α_Q and β respectively for the three conditions, the result on differentiation (compare (2.12)) is:

$$\sum_j (-\ln n_j^* + \alpha_P + \beta \varepsilon_j) \, dn_j$$

$$+ \sum_k (-\ln n_k'^* + \alpha_Q + \beta \varepsilon_k') \, dn_k = 0.$$

The Lagrange method then enables one to see that, for the appropriate values of the three multipliers, each term in the two sums is separately equal to zero, so that the final result is for system P:

$$n_j^* = \exp(\alpha_P + \beta \varepsilon_j)$$

and for system Q:

$$n_k'^* = \exp(\alpha_Q + \beta\varepsilon_k').$$

Where does this leave us? What it shows is that both system P and system Q have their thermal equilibrium distributions of the Boltzmann type (compare equation (2.12)). The distributions have their own private values of α, and we can see from the derivation that this followed from the introduction of the separate conditions for particle conservation (equations (2.16) and (2.17)). However, the two distributions have the same value of β. This arose in the derivation from the single energy condition (2.18), in other words from the thermal contact or energy interchange between the systems. So the important conclusion is that two systems in mutual thermal equilibrium have distributions with the same β. From thermodynamics we know that they necessarily have the same empiric temperature, and thus the same thermodynamic temperature T. Therefore it follows that β *is a function of* T *only*.

2.3.2 Temperature and entropy

We now come to the form of this relation β and T. The simplest approach is to know the answer(!), and we shall choose to *define* a statistical temperature in terms of β from the equation

$$\beta = -1/k_B T. \tag{2.20}$$

What will eventually become clear (notably when we discuss ideal gases in Chapter 6) is that this definition of T does indeed agree with the absolute thermodynamic scale of temperature. Meanwhile we shall adopt equation (2.20) knowing that its justification will follow.

There is much similarity with our early definition of entropy as $S = k_B \ln \Omega$, introduced in section 1.7. And in fact the connection between these two results is something well worth exploring at this stage, particularly since it can give us a microscopic picture of heat and work in reversible processes.

Consider how the internal energy U of a system can be changed. From a macroscopic viewpoint, this can be done by adding heat and/or work, i.e. change in U = heat input + work input. The laws of thermodynamics for a differential change in a simple P–V system tell us that:

$$dU = TdS - PdV \qquad (2.21)$$

where for reversible processes (only) the first (TdS) term can be identified as the heat input, and the second term ($-PdV$) as the work input.

Now let us consider the microscopic picture. The internal energy is simply the sum of energies of all the particles of the system, i.e. $U = \sum n_j \varepsilon_j$. Taking again a differential change in U, we obtain:

$$dU = \sum_j \varepsilon_j dn_j + \sum_j n_j d\varepsilon_j \qquad (2.22)$$

where the first term allows for changes in the occupation numbers n_j, and the second term for changes in the energy levels ε_j.

It is not hard to convince oneself that the respective first and second terms of equations (2.21) and (2.22) match up. The energy levels are dependent only on V, so that a $-PdV$ work input can only address the second term of (2.22). And, bearing in mind the correlation between S and Ω (and hence t^*, and hence $\{n_j^*\}$), it is equally clear that occupation number changes are directly related to entropy changes. Hence the matching up of the first terms. These ideas turn out to be both interesting and useful. The relation $-PdV = \sum n_j d\varepsilon_j$ gives a direct and physical way of calculating the pressure from a microscopic model. And the other relation bears directly on the topic of this section.

The argument in outline is as follows. Start by considering how a change in $\ln \Omega$ can be brought about:

$$d(\ln \Omega) = d(\ln t^*) \qquad \text{for a large system}$$
$$= -\sum_j \ln n_j^* dn_j \qquad \text{as in equation (2.7)}$$

$$= -\sum_j (\alpha + \beta\varepsilon_j)\,\mathrm{d}n_j \qquad \text{using the Boltz-} \atop \text{mann distribution}$$

$$= -\beta\sum_j \varepsilon_j\,\mathrm{d}n_j \qquad \text{since } N \text{ is fixed}$$

$$= -\beta(\mathrm{d}U)_{\text{no work}} \qquad \text{first term of equation (2.22)}$$

$$= -\beta(T\,\mathrm{d}S) \qquad \text{first term of equation (2.21).}$$

This identification is consistent with $S = k_B \ln \Omega$ together with $\beta = -1/k_B T$. It shows clearly that the two statistical definitions are linked, i.e. that equation (2.20) validates equation (1.5) or vice versa. Part of this consistency is to note that it must be the same constant (k_B, Boltzmann's constant) which appears in both definitions.

2.4 The Boltzmann distribution and the partition function

We now return to discuss the Boltzmann distribution. We have seen that this distribution is the appropriate one to describe the thermal equilibrium properties of an assembly of N identical localized (distinguishable) weakly interacting particles. We have derived it for an isolated assembly having a fixed volume V and a fixed internal energy U. An important part in the result is played by the parameter β which is a function of the macrostate (U, V, N). However, the upshot of the previous section is to note that the Boltzmann distribution is most easily written and understood in terms of (T, V, N) rather than (U, V, N). This is no inconvenience, since it frequently happens in practice that it is T rather than U that is known. And it is no embarrassment from a fundamental point of view so long as we are dealing with a large enough system that fluctuations are unimportant. Therefore, although our method logically determines T (and other thermodynamic quantities) as a function of (U, V, N) for an isolated system, we shall usually use the results to describe the behaviour of U (and other thermodynamic quantities) as a function of (T, V, N). (This subject will be reopened in the final three chapters of the book.)

Therefore, we now write the Boltzmann distribution as:

$$n_j = (N/Z) \exp\left(- \varepsilon_j/k_B T\right) \tag{2.23}$$

with the partition function Z defined as:

$$Z = \sum_j \exp\left(- \varepsilon_j/k_B T\right). \tag{2.24}$$

(From now on we shall for simplicity omit the *s from n_j, since all the discussion will relate to thermal equilibrium.) It is worth making two points about the partition function. The first is that its common symbol Z is used from the German word for sum-over-states, for that is all the partition function is: the sum over all one-particle states of the 'Boltzmann factors' $\exp\left(- \varepsilon_j/k_B T\right)$. The second point concerns its English name. It is called the partition function because (in thermal equilibrium at temperature T) n_j is proportional to the corresponding term in the sum. In other words the N particles are partitioned into their possible states (labelled by j) in just the same ratios as Z is split up into the Boltzmann factor terms. In a formula:

$$n_j/N = \exp\left(- \varepsilon_j/k_B T\right)/Z \tag{2.25}$$

or $\quad n_j/n_k = \exp\left[- (\varepsilon_j - \varepsilon_k)/k_B T\right]. \tag{2.26}$

In fact the way of writing the Boltzmann distribution given in (2.26) is a very straightforward way of remembering it. And expressions of the type $\exp\left(- \Delta \varepsilon/k_B T\right)$ turn up in all sorts of different physical situations.

2.5 Calculation of thermodynamic functions

To finish this chapter we discuss a few practicalities about how the Boltzmann distribution may be used to calculate thermodynamic functions from first principles. In the next chapter we apply these ideas to two particular physical cases.

We start with our system at given (T, V, N) as discussed in the previous section. There are then (at least) three useful routes for calculation. The best one to use will depend on which thermodynamic functions are to be calculated–and there is no substitute for experience in deciding!

Method 1: Use $S = k_B \ln \Omega$

This method is often the shortest to use if only the entropy is required. The point is that one can substitute the Boltzmann distribution numbers (equation (2.23)) back into the expression (2.3) in order to give t^* and hence Ω (equation (2.4)) and hence S. Thus S is obtained from a knowledge of the ε_js (which depend on V), of N and of T (as it enters the Boltzmann distribution).

Method 2: Use the definition of Z

There is a direct shortcut from the partition function to U. This is particularly useful if only U and perhaps dU/dT ($= C_V$ the heat capacity at constant volume) are wanted. In fact U can be worked out at once from $U = \sum n_j \varepsilon_j$, but this sum can be neatly performed by looking back at equation (2.15), which can be re-expressed as:

$$(U/N) = (1/Z)\,dZ/d\beta = d(\ln Z)/d\beta. \qquad (2.27)$$

Note that it is usually convenient to retain β as the variable here rather than to use T.

Method 3: The 'royal route'

This one never fails, so it is worth knowing! The route uses the Helmholtz free energy F, defined as $F = U - TS$. The reason for the importance of the method is two-fold. First, the statistical calculation of F turns out to be extremely simple from the Boltzmann distribution. The calculation goes as follows:

$$F = U - TS \qquad \text{definition}$$

$$= \sum n_j \varepsilon_j - k_B T \ln t^* \qquad \text{statistical } U \text{ and } S$$

$$= \sum n_j \varepsilon_j - k_B T (N \ln N - \sum n_j \ln n_j) \qquad \text{using equation (2.6) with } \sum n_j = N$$

$$= -N k_B T \ln Z, \text{ simply.} \qquad \text{using Boltzmann on } \ln n_j \quad (2.28)$$

In the last step one takes the logarithm of (2.23) to obtain $\ln n_j = \ln N - \ln Z - \varepsilon_j/k_B T$. Everything but the $\ln Z$ term cancels, giving the memorable and simple result (2.28).

The second reason for following this route is that an expression for F in terms of (T, V, N) is of immediate use in thermodynamics since (T, V, N) are the natural co-ordinates for F (e.g. see *Thermal Physics* by Finn, Ch. 10). In fact $dF = -SdT - PdV + \mu dN$, so that simple differentiation can give S, P and the chemical potential μ at once; and most other quantities can also be derived with little effort. We shall see how these ideas work out in the next chapter.

Chapter 3
Two examples

We now apply the general results of the previous chapter to two specific examples, chosen because they are easily soluble mathematically, whilst yet being of direct relevance to real physical systems. The first example is an assembly whose localized particles have just two possible states. In the second the particles are harmonic oscillators.

3.1 A spin-$\frac{1}{2}$ solid

First we derive the statistical physics of an assembly whose particles have just two states. Then we apply the results to an ideal 'spin-$\frac{1}{2}$ solid'. Finally we can examine briefly how far this model describes the observed properties of real substances, particularly in the realm of ultra-low temperature physics.

3.1.1 An assembly of particles with two states

Consider an assembly of N localized weakly interacting particles in which there are just two one-particle states. We label these states $j = 0$ and $j = 1$, with energies (under given conditions) ε_0 and ε_1. The results of the previous chapter can be used to write down expressions for the properties of the assembly at given temperature T.

The distribution numbers

The partition function Z (equation (2.24)) has only two terms. It is $Z = \exp\left(-\varepsilon_0/k_\mathrm{B}T\right) + \exp\left(-\varepsilon_1/k_\mathrm{B}T\right)$, which can be conveniently written as:

$$Z = \exp\left(- \varepsilon_0/k_B T\right) \left[1 + \exp\left(- \varepsilon/k_B T\right)\right] \quad (3.1)$$

where the energy ε is defined as the difference between the energy levels $(\varepsilon_1 - \varepsilon_0)$. We may note that equation (3.1) may be written as $Z = Z(0) \times Z(\text{th})$, the product of two factors. The first factor $(Z(0) = \exp\left(- \varepsilon_0/k_B T\right)$, the so-called zero-point term) depends only on the ground-state energy ε_0, whereas the second factor $(Z(\text{th})$, the thermal term) depends only on the relative energy ε between the two levels.

The thermal equilibrium distribution numbers (or occupation numbers) n_0 and n_1 may now be evaluated from equation (2.23) to give:

$$n_0 = N/[1 + \exp\left(- \varepsilon/k_B T\right)] = N/Z(\text{th})$$

and $\quad n_1 = N \exp\left(- \varepsilon/k_B T\right)/[1 + \exp\left(- \varepsilon/k_B T\right)]$

$$= N \exp\left(- \varepsilon/k_B T\right)/Z(\text{th}). \quad (3.2)$$

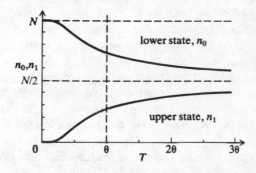

Fig. 3.1 Occupation numbers for the two states of a spin-$\frac{1}{2}$ solid in thermal equilibrium at temperature T. The characteristic temperature θ depends only on the energy difference between the two states. The particles are all in the lower state when $T \ll \theta$, but the occupation of the two states becomes equal when $T \gg \theta$.

These numbers are sketched in Fig. 3.1 as functions of T. We can note the following points:

1. The numbers $n_{0,1}$ do not depend at all on the ground state energy ε_0. The first factor $Z(0)$ of equation (3.1)

does not enter at all. Instead all the relevant information is contained in Z(th). This should cause no surprise since all is contained in the simple statement (2.26) of the Boltzmann distribution, namely $n_1/n_0 = \exp(-\varepsilon/k_BT)$, together with $n_0 + n_1 = N$. Hence also:

2. The numbers $n_{0,1}$ are functions only of ε/k_BT. One can think of this as the ratio of two 'energy scales'. One scale ε represents the separation between the two energy levels of the particles, and is determined by the applied conditions, e.g. of volume V (or for our spin-$\frac{1}{2}$ solid of applied magnetic field–see later). The second energy scale is k_BT, which should be thought of as *a thermal energy scale*. Equivalently, the variable may be written as θ/T, the ratio of two temperatures, where $\theta = \varepsilon/k_B$ is a temperature characteristic of the energy-level spacing. This idea of temperature or energy scales turns out to be valuable in many other situations also.

3. At low temperatures (meaning $T \ll \theta$, or equivalently $k_BT \ll \varepsilon$), equation (3.2) gives $n_0 = N$, $n_1 = 0$. To employ useful picture language, all the particles are frozen out into the lowest energy (ground) state, and none is excited into the higher state.

4. On the other hand at high temperatures (meaning $T \gg \theta$ or $k_BT \gg \varepsilon$) we have $n_0 = n_1 = N/2$. There are equal numbers in the two states, i.e. the difference in energy between them has become an irrelevance. The probability of any particle being in either of the two states is the same, just like in the penny-tossing problem of Appendix 2.

Internal energy U

An expression for U can be written down at once as:

$$U = n_0 \varepsilon_0 + n_1 \varepsilon_1$$
$$= N\varepsilon_0 + n_1 \varepsilon \qquad (3.3)$$

with n_1 given by equation (3.2). This function is sketched in Fig. 3.2. The first term in equation (3.3) is the 'zero-point' energy, $U(0)$, the energy $T = 0$. The second term is the

Fig. 3.2 The variation of internal energy with temperature for spin-$\frac{1}{2}$ solid. $U(0)$ is the zero-point energy.

'thermal energy', $U(\text{th})$, which depends on the energy level spacing ε and k_BT only.

One should note that the expression may also be obtained directly from the partition function (3.1) using equation (2.27). The $Z(0)$ factor leads to $U(0)$ and the $Z(\text{th})$ factor to the $U(\text{th})$. It is seen from Fig. 3.2 that the transition from low to high temperature behaviour again occurs around the characteristic temperature θ.

Heat capacity C

The heat capacity C (strictly C_V, or in general the heat capacity at constant energy levels) is obtained by differentiating U with respect to T. The zero-point term goes out, and one obtains:

$$C = Nk_B \frac{(\theta/T)^2 \exp(-\theta/T)}{[1 + \exp(-\theta/T)]^2}. \tag{3.4}$$

The result, plotted in Fig. 3.3, shows a substantial maximum (of order Nk_B, the natural unit for C) at a temperature near to θ. C vanishes rapidly (as $\exp(-\varepsilon/k_BT)/T^2$) at low temperatures. It also goes to zero, albeit rather more gently as $1/T^2$, at high temperatures. (Prove this last statement? Seen by expanding the exponentials in equation (3.4).)

Fig. 3.3 The variation of heat capacity with temperature for a spin-$\frac{1}{2}$ solid, showing the peak of the Schottky anomaly (see section 3.1.2).

Entropy S

Finally we obtain the entropy S. Again this is a thermal property only, independent of the zero-point term. With section 2.5 before us we have three possible derivations. Method 1 can be used (together with Stirling's approximation) to give the answer from the distribution numbers (3.2) without recourse to calculus. Alternatively (method 2) one can obtain S from an integration of C up from the absolute zero (since $S = 0$ there), i.e. $S = \int_0 (C/T)\, dT$. This is possible but not recommended. Instead let us use method 3. From equation (2.28) we write down

$$F = -Nk_B T \ln Z$$

$$= N\varepsilon_0 - Nk_B T \ln\left[1 + \exp\left(-\varepsilon/k_B T\right)\right] \tag{3.5}$$

substituting equation (3.1) for Z. Again note the zero-point and thermal terms in equation (3.5). The entropy is obtained by one differentiation, since $S = -(\partial F/\partial T)_{V,N}$, the differentiation being at constant energy levels and number. The result:

$$S = Nk_B \left\{ \ln\left[1 + \exp\left(-\theta/T\right)\right] \right.$$
$$\left. + \frac{(\theta/T)\exp\left(-\theta/T\right)}{\left[1 + \exp\left(-\theta/T\right)\right]} \right\} \tag{3.6}$$

is illustrated in Fig. 3.4.

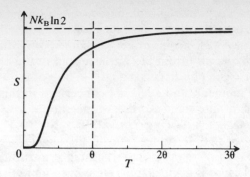

Fig. 3.4 The variation of entropy with temperature for a spin-$\frac{1}{2}$ solid. Note the transition from perfect order ($S = 0$) towards total disorder ($S = Nk_B \ln 2$).

The high and low temperature values of S are worth noting. When $T \ll \theta$, S is again frozen out exponentially towards the value 0 which it must attain eventually (the Third Law!). As $T \to 0$ all the particles enter the ground state, and the assembly becomes completely ordered (i.e. $\Omega = 1$). At high temperatures, however, the particles are randomized between the two states, so that $\Omega = 2^N$, and S reaches the expected value $Nk_B \ln 2$ (again like the penny tossing problem). The approach to the high T limit again goes as $1/T^2$.

3.1.2 Magnetic solids

Actually the two-state situation is quite a common one. It occurs because of the existence of spin states in atoms. If a single atom has an angular momentum quantum number of $\frac{1}{2}$, then when it experiences a magnetic field B, the atomic energy levels split into two. One level goes up by μB and the other goes down by μB, where μ is the z-component of the magnetic moment associated with the angular momentum. This is the Zeeman effect (much loved by spectroscopists, since this splitting of $2\mu B$ can be observed by a variety of techniques). In the lowest (ground) state one can imagine the atomic moment to be aligned parallel to the field, whereas in the upper (unstable) state it is antiparallel.

There are two origins of these magnetic moments in solids. One is from the electrons in the atom, and the other from the nucleus. An electronic effect can come both from the orbital motion and also from the intrinsic spin of the electron. The precise value of μ depends on the details of the atomic origin of the moment, and need not concern us in this discussion, except to note that in order of magnitude it will equal the *Bohr magneton* μ_B $(= e\hbar/2m = 0.93 \times 10^{-23} \text{ J T}^{-1})$. For simplicity we shall in future refer to the angular momentum as 'spin', regardless of its actual orbital or intrinsic origin. The second cause is nuclear spin. Here even more the magnitude of μ depends on the specific nucleus, but the much smaller order of magnitude is the *nuclear magneton* μ_N $(= e\hbar/2M_P = 5.05 \times 10^{-27} \text{ J T}^{-1})$.

We now consider the thermal properties of a solid whose atoms have spin $\frac{1}{2}$. To whatever properties the solid would exhibit without the $2\mu B$ splitting, we must add a spin contribution. And in many situations this contribution is precisely described by the two-state model of the previous section. In order for our model to apply, all we require is that the localized spins are weakly interacting and identical. This is a good approximation if (but only if) the spins are sufficiently far apart that the B-field experienced by each spin arises almost entirely from an externally applied field, rather than from the influence of its neighbours. In the usual terminology this means that the substance is paramagnetic (alignment of permanent moments in an applied field) rather than ferromagnetic or antiferromagnetic (spontaneous alignment of permanent moments). Another profitable way of stating the requirement is that the energy levels ε_0 and ε_1 do not themselves depend on the occupation numbers n_0 and n_1, but only on the applied field. This is a good approximation for most nuclear spin systems, since μ_N is small. It applies only to a limited range of electronic spin systems, notably diluted paramagnetic salts such as cerium magnesium nitrate (CMN) which contains only a few spins (Ce^{3+} ions) separated by a lot of non-magnetic padding (all the other atoms, including water of crystallization).

For this type of ideal paramagnetic substance the hard work is already done. (A treatment of ferromagnetism appears later, in Chapter 11.) We may use the results of section 3.1.1 to determine the contribution of the spins to the thermal properties of the solid. The energy difference ε between the two states is equal to $2\mu B$, and hence the characteristic temperature θ equals $2\mu B/k_B$. The number N is the number of spin-$\frac{1}{2}$ particles in the solid (i.e. much less than the number of atoms in the case of CMN). Note the following:

1. The thermal properties of the spins, dependent only on θ/T, are thus for a given system universal functions of B/T. We shall use this result for S in particular in the next section.
2. Typical values of θ in strong magnetic fields are a few degrees K for an electronic spin system, but a few mK for a nuclear spin system. As we shall see later in the book, there are few other thermal contributions at such low temperatures, so that the spins in fact form the major thermal bath in the solid.
3. We are restricting our discussion to a spin-$\frac{1}{2}$ solid, one which has just two spin states. The treatment for a higher spin follows very similar lines, with qualitatively identical results. The major difference is that, since a spin I has $(2I+1)$ possible states, the high temperature entropy is $Nk_B \ln (2I+1)$ rather than $Nk_B \ln 2$. The general form of all the functions is similar, with again a characteristic temperature θ which relates to the Zeeman splitting.
4. The heat capacity (Fig. 3.3) is worthy of note. Heat capacities of this sort are called Schottky anomalies. The word 'anomalies' is used because of the potential upset to an unsuspecting experimenter. As the range of measurement is reduced below room temperature, the large lattice contribution to a typical solid heat capacity reduces rapidly (often as T^3) towards zero. Imagine the consternation when a further reduction of T sees an *increasing*

T^{-2} contribution starting to come in! However, this is precisely what happens as spins in the system become ordered as θ is reached.

3.1.3 Cooling by adiabatic demagnetization

The paramagnetic solid can form the basis of a method of cooling, and one which is of great importance in physics, since it is the only workable method in the sub-millikelvin region.

The theory of the method is easily followed from an $S-T$ diagram as shown in Fig. 3.5. The figure shows two entropy curves, one in the highest available field (B_1), and one in a low field (B_2). As noted above, S is a function only of B/T, so the only difference between the two curves is the scaling along the T-axis. The cooling method uses two distinct steps. Firstly the solid is magnetized at the lowest available precooling temperature, T_1. This is illustrated in Fig. 3.5 by the step AB, which represents an isothermal magnetization.

Fig. 3.5 Cooling by adiabatic magnetization. The two $S-T$ curves give the behaviour in a high magnetic field B_1, and a low field, B_2, AB represents the precooling process (removal of entropy at a high temperature), and BC the adiabatic demagnetization to the final temperature T_2.

In the second step, the system is then thermally isolated and the magnetic field gradually reduced, giving an adiabatic reversible (i.e. isentropic) process. In other words the system goes from B to C on the diagram, and its temperature reduces from T_1 to T_2. (Actually the spin-$\frac{1}{2}$ solid is a very suitable working substance for a refrigerator–the requirements are that S should vary with T and with another control parameter. Here the parameter is the applied magnetic field; in a more common fluid refrigerator it is the pressure.)

It is interesting to consider the two processes microscopically. In the isothermal magnetization leg (AB), the spins tend to align in the strong magnetic field since μB is comparable to $k_B T$. In this process, the population of the lower state (energy $-\mu B$, i.e. with μ parallel to B) grows at the expense of the upper state (energy $+\mu B$). The population becomes (somewhat) ordered, and the entropy decreases. During this process heat of magnetization is evolved from the system, and in fact the precooling refrigerator has to be very active to maintain the temperature at T_1. In the second adiabatic step (BC), the situation is different. The spins are no longer in contact with a heat bath, so the occupation numbers cannot change. As discussed in Chapter 2, S constant means $t(\{n_j\})$ constant which means $\{n_j\}$ constant. Hence at C the occupation numbers $n_{0,1}$ are just the same as they were at B. However, the energy level spacing has reduced (from $2\mu B_1$ to $2\mu B_2$) and so the temperature must have also decreased in the same ratio, in order to keep $\mu B/k_B T$ constant. Therefore the cooling obeys the simple law:

$$T_2 = T_1 \ (B_2/B_1). \tag{3.7}$$

This is a nice example of the importance of entropy. In the first leg we reduce the entropy of the solid at a high temperature by an amount ΔS, say, by extracting a quantity $T_1 \Delta S$ of heat. The adiabatic leg then transfers the entropy reduction to a lower temperature, and the spins can absorb heat of at least $T_2 \Delta S$ from their surroundings before warming up again to the starting point. (More accurately the amount of cooling available from the spins equals the area between the entropy curve and the S axis between points C and A, i.e. $\int_C^A T \, dS$).

Some experimental details

We shall refer to two implementations of the cooling method. One is the use of CMN to cool to about 2 mK, and the second is the use of Cu nuclei to cool into the μK region.

The necessary starting conditions are easy to work out. To obtain a significant entropy reduction ΔS under the starting conditions, one requires μB_1 to be of the same order of magnitude as $k_B T_1$. In the case of electronic moments (CMN), this requirement is comfortably attained with a precooling temperature T_1 of around 1 K and an applied field B_1 of 1 T. For nuclear moments (Cu) the starting conditions are more stringent by a factor of over 1000. They are marginally met in modern techniques using almost the highest available magnetic field–typically a 7 T superconducting magnet, and a precooling refrigerator operating at around 10 mK. Even so only a few per cent of the copper spin entropy is removed.

The essential ingredients are indicated in Fig. 3.6. For CMN the precooling stage is usually a pumped helium cryostat (reaching about 1 K with ^{4}He, or 0.3 K with ^{3}He).

Fig. 3.6 A schematic apparatus for cooling by adiabatic demagnetization.

For nuclear spins it will be a 'dilution refrigerator', a device capable of reaching 3–10 mK whose working substance is a ^{3}He–^{4}He mixture which phase separates at temperatures below 0.7 K. The magnet nowadays would be a superconducting solenoid operated in the main helium bath for both experiments.

The CMN coolant is often in the form of a powdered slurry around a bunch of fine copper wires for thermal contact. The active particles for nuclear cooling are the ^{63}Cu and ^{65}Cu nuclei in copper metal (both of these nuclei having spin $\frac{3}{2}$). The copper is in the form of wires, plates or powder.

The final element in the experiment is the heat switch and thermal link. We require an arrangement which will give excellent thermal contact in the precooling stage (A → B) but which can give near perfect isolation in the adiabatic cooling stage (B → C). Mechanical systems give too much frictional heating, and use of low pressure He gas as a heat exchange medium has serious drawbacks (e.g. it is difficult to remove for the second stage). The modern solution is to use a thermal link of high-conductivity metal (silver or copper) broken by a superconducting heat switch. This consists of a pure metal (aluminium or tin) which is a superconductor. When a (fairly small) magnetic field is applied to the switch, the superconductivity is destroyed and the metal is a good conductor of heat, as wanted in the precooling leg. However, when this field is removed and the switch becomes superconducting, it becomes a very poor conductor of heat–the superconducting electrons move in an ordered way, so that although they carry charge without resistance they have no entropy to carry! A superconducting heat switch can have a conductance ratio of 10^5 or higher at 10 mK.

Suppose we wish to cool liquid ^{3}He into the μK temperature region, a worthwhile task since it becomes a 'superfluid' below 1–2 mK. Clearly we can use the arrangement of Fig. 3.6 to cool some Cu spins. The major technical problem remaining is to achieve adequate thermal contact between the Cu spins and the sample of liquid ^{3}He. And this turns out to be the most severe problem of all. The trick is to cut down extraneous heat inputs (to the pW level) with antivibration measures and with careful electrical screening, and also to maximize the area of contact between the copper metal and the liquid with ultrafine sintered silver power. In this way it is possible at the time of writing to achieve helium temperatures of about $100\,\mu$K.

What limits the final temperature?

This is a question worth asking. The problem can be stated simply. If I take equation (3.7) seriously, then is it not possible to make the final temperature T_2 as small as I wish, simply by reducing B_2 to zero? In fact can the spins not be cooled to the absolute zero?

The answer is 'no, they cannot', one of many ways of stating the Third Law of thermodynamics. And the reason lies in the meaning of equation (3.7). That equation arose from the fact that the occupation numbers must be unchanged in an adiabatic process, i.e. that $2\mu B/k_B T$ must remain at a fixed value. The numerator $2\mu B$ is the energy level spacing ε, and it is this quantity which cannot reach zero. The two spin states can never have the same energy ('the ground state of a system can never be degenerate' might be another way of stating the Third Law). Instead there will always be some residual interactions left, even if these are only magnetic dipole–dipole forces between the N spins. As remarked earlier, although our treatment neglects interactions between particles some interactions are essential, otherwise thermal equilibrium could never be reached: hence 'weakly interacting'. We may turn off the externally applied magnetic field (B_0 say), but some residual interactions must remain. If we characterize these by an effective field (B_{int}), then the B entering equations such as (3.7) should be the appropriate sum of B_0 and B_{int}. Bearing in mind the random direction of B_{int}, the correct expression is:

$$B = (B_0{}^2 + B_{int}{}^2)^{\frac{1}{2}}. \tag{3.8}$$

The energy levels obtained from equation (3.8) are plotted in Fig. 3.7.

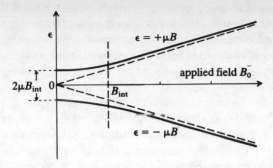

Fig. 3.7 The energies of a spin-$\frac{1}{2}$ solid as a function of applied magnetic field B_0.

The upshot of all this on the lowest final temperature is:

1. The absolute zero is unattainable; the temperature reached in zero final applied field is $T_1(B_{int}/B_1)$, a non-zero number.

2. Another way of expressing this result is to observe that the spins will order in zero applied field at around a temperature $T_{int} = \mu B_{int}/k_B$. Referring back to Fig. 3.5, the entropy does not stay at $Nk_B \ln 2$ as T is lowered past this value, but falls to zero to achieve $S = 0$ at $T = 0$.

3. Since the cooling method is useful only around $\mu B/k_B T \sim 1$, the lowest attainable practical temperature is around T_{int}. For CMN this is about 1 mK, a very low value for an electronic spin system; hence the importance of this particular salt. For Cu spins in the pure metal, T_{int} is less than 0.1 μK, one of the reasons for its choice.

3.1.4 Magnetization and thermometry

Before leaving the topic of the spin-$\frac{1}{2}$ solid we discuss its magnetic properties. These may be readily derived from the Boltzmann distribution, and they give a convenient method for measuring the low temperatures reached by adiabatic demagnetization. Without labouring the point, it is no accident that the working substance of a refrigerator is also a possible candidate for thermometry–the refrigerant must have S a strong function of T, i.e. it must be thermally active ('doing something') in that temperature range!

Magnetization

We characterize the magnetic properties by the magnetic moment M of the whole assembly of N spins. Interactions will be neglected, at any rate until we discuss ferromagnetism much later in the book, so that B may be taken as the externally applied field. In the lower state, each spin has a component μ aligned to the B field, whereas each spin in the upper state has a component $-\mu$. And the numbers of spins in the two states in thermal equilibrium at temperature T are given by the Boltzmann distribution, equation (3.2). Hence we have:

$$M = n_0(\mu) + n_1(-\mu)$$
$$= N\mu[\exp(\mu B/k_B T) - \exp(-\mu B/k_B T)]/$$
$$[\exp(\mu B/k_B T) + \exp(-\mu B/k_B T)]$$
$$= N\mu \tanh(\mu B/k_B T). \tag{3.9}$$

This expression is plotted in Fig. 3.8, and one can note:

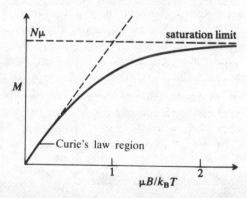

Fig. 3.8 The magnetization of a spin-$\frac{1}{2}$ solid as a (universal) function of $\mu B/k_B T$.

1. At high enough B, or low enough T, the magnetization saturates at the value $N\mu$, an obvious result since then all the N spins have aligned with the field.
2. For a solid with a higher spin (like the spin-$\frac{3}{2}$ Cu nuclei) the shape of the curve is superficially similar, although it is not a simple tanh function.
3. In the weakly paramagnetic limit, i.e. $\mu B/k_B T \ll 1$, at low fields or high temperatures, then the curve is essentially linear and we have:

$$M = N\mu(\mu B/k_B T).\tag{3.10}$$

This result may readily be verified by expanding the exponentials in equation (3.9), bearing in mind that the exponents $\pm\mu B$ are small. Hence in this limit the magnetic susceptibility, essentially M/B, is proportional to $1/T$. This is *Curie's Law*.

Therefore we have a direct $1/T$ thermometer. For an electronic paramagnet like CMN, the magnetization is usually measured directly from the total magnetization of the solid. The usual method is to measure the mutual inductance between two coils, wound over the CMN, giving a constant reading (which can be subtracted) and a component proportional to $1/T$. This may be used as a thermometer from 10 K or higher to around 1 mK, where interactions take over and spoil the simple story. Below about 20 mK, however, a nulear system (often Pt nuclei) becomes useful. However, the value of μ is so small that the direct method is impractical—one would measure the effect of minute magnetic impurities with electronic spins. Therefore a resonance method is used (pulsed NMR) which singles out the particular energy level splitting of interest by means of radio frequency photons of the correct frequency. The strength of the NMR signal is directly proportional to $1/T$.

3.2 Localized harmonic oscillators

A second example which can be solved with little computational difficulty is that of an assembly of N localized harmonic oscillators. Suppose the oscillators are each free to move in one dimension only and that they each have the same classical frequency ν. They are therefore identical localized particles, and the results of Chapter 2 may be used to describe the equilibrium properties of the assembly at temperature T.

First we need the result from quantum mechanics for the states of one particle. For a simple harmonic oscillator there is an infinite number of possible states $(j = 0, 1, 2, 3 \ldots)$ whose energies are given by:

$$\varepsilon_j = (j + \tfrac{1}{2})h\nu. \tag{3.11}$$

(Most books on quantum mechanics, e.g. Davies's book, *Quantum Mechanics*, in this series Chapter 3, include a discussion of the states of a harmonic oscillator, if you are not familiar with the problem.)

3.2.1 The thermal properties

There is an infinite number of states given by equation (3.11), and therefore an infinite number of terms in the partition function Z. Nevertheless the even spacing of the energy levels enables Z to be summed explicitly as a geometric progression. We have:

$$Z = \sum_j \exp\left[-(j + \tfrac{1}{2})h\nu/k_{\mathrm{B}}T\right] \qquad \text{from equations (2.24) and (3.11)}$$

$$= \sum_j \exp\left[-(j + \tfrac{1}{2})\theta/T\right] \qquad \text{defining } \theta \text{ from } h\nu = k_{\mathrm{B}}\theta$$

$$= \exp(-\theta/2T)\cdot\sum_j \exp(-j\theta/T) \qquad \text{separating the common factor}$$

$$= \exp(-\theta/2T) \\ \cdot[1 - \exp(-\theta/T)]^{-1} \qquad \text{doing the sum (see below!)}$$

$$= Z(0)\cdot Z(\text{th}) \qquad \text{say, compare equation (3.1)}$$

$$\tag{3.12}$$

The evaluation of the sum in the $Z(\text{th})$ factor above is straightforward. If we write $y = \exp(-h\nu/k_B T)$, then the required sum is $(1 + y + y^2 + y^3 + \cdots)$, which is readily summed to infinity to give $(1 - y)^{-1}$. (Check it by multiplying both sides by $1 - y$ if you are unsure). The separation in equation (3.12) into a zero-point term $Z(0)$ and a thermal term $Z(\text{th})$ has a similar significance to our earlier factorization of equation (3.1).

Now that Z is evaluated in terms of T and the oscillators' scale temperature θ, there is no problem in working out expressions for the thermal quantities. For example, U is obtained by taking logarithms of equation (3.12) and differentiating as in equation (2.27). The result:

$$U = \tfrac{1}{2}Nh\nu + \frac{Nh\nu}{\exp(\theta/T) - 1} \tag{3.13}$$

is plotted in Fig. 3.9. The first term is the zero-point energy, derived from $Z(0)$, and the second term the thermal energy

Fig. 3.9 The variation of internal energy with temperature for an assembly of harmonic oscillators. The characteristic temperature θ depends on the frequency of the oscillators (see text). Note the high and low temperature limits.

arising from $Z(\text{th})$. At high temperatures, as the figure demonstrates, the internal energy becomes

$$U = Nk_{\text{B}}T \tag{3.14}$$

to a rather high degree of accuracy. (Expand the exponential in (3.13) to test this!) We return below to this simple but important expression.

The heat capacity is obtained by differentiating equation (3.13):

$$C = \frac{dU}{dT} = Nk_B \frac{(\theta/T)^2 \exp(\theta/T)}{[\exp(\theta/T) - 1]^2}. \tag{3.15}$$

This is plotted in Fig. 3.10, and as expected from equation (3.14) one may observe that $C = Nk_B$ at high temperatures ($T > \theta$).

Fig. 3.10 The variation of heat capacity with temperature for an assembly of harmonic oscillators.

The entropy S is also readily derived, the easiest route again being to evaluate F (equation (2.28)) and to differentiate F with respect to T. The result is

$$S = Nk_B \left[\ln\left(\frac{\exp(\theta/T)}{\exp(\theta/T) - 1} \right) + \frac{(\theta/T)}{(\exp(\theta/T) - 1)} \right]. \tag{3.16}$$

The reader may wish to check that the low temperature limit is $S = 0$ (no surprise), and that at high temperatures the expression becomes $S = Nk_B \ln(T/\theta) = Nk_B \ln(k_B T/h\nu)$.

3.2.2 The extreme quantum and the classical limits

The assembly of localized oscillators forms a good example of the use of $k_B T$ as the thermal energy scale.

Firstly consider the oscillators at an extremely low temperature, i.e. $T \ll \theta$ or $k_B T \ll h\nu$. The oscillators are frozen into the ground state, in that virtually none is thermally excited at any one time. We have $U = U(0)$, $C = 0$, $S = 0$. This situation should be thought of as the 'extreme quantum limit'. The discrete (i.e. quantum) nature of the states given by equation (3.11) is totally dominating the properties

However, at the opposite extreme of temperature, i.e. $T \gg \theta$ or $k_B T \gg h\nu$, we reach a 'classical limit'. In this limit the simple expressions for U and C involve only $k_B T$ and *not* $h\nu$. Planck's constant, i.e. the scale of the energy level splitting, is irrelevant now. Oscillators of any frequency have the same average energy $k_B T$. This dependence of U on $k_B T$ alone is associated with the old classical 'law of equipartition of energy', which states that each so-called degree of freedom of a system contributes $\frac{1}{2} k_B T$ to the internal energy. In this case each oscillator displays two degrees of freedom (one for its kinetic energy and one for its potential energy), and the old law gives the result $U = N k_B T$ for the N oscillators. But the question left unanswered by the classical law alone is: When is a degree of freedom excited and when is it frozen out? The answer is in the energy (or temperature) scales! We shall return to these ideas in our discussions of gases in Chapters 6 and 7.

Before leaving this topic, let us examine the entropy S. One can see from equation (3.16) that even in the classical limit, the expression for S involves h, Planck's constant. Entropy is fundamentally a quantum effect. From the classical region alone one can deduce that $S = S_0 + N k_B \ln T$, but there is no way of finding the constant S_0 without integrating the thermal properties upwards from $T = 0$, i.e. through the quantum region. This problem lies at the heart of a number of the historical paradoxes and controversies of classical statistical mechanics in the pre-quantum age.

This quantum nature of S is well illustrated from a microscopic interpretation of equation (3.16). If one has an assembly of particles, each of which may be in G states with equal probability, then S is readily evaluated. ($G = 2$ is the spin-$\frac{1}{2}$ solid at high temperatures, for example, and we used $G = 4$ for Cu nuclei having spin $\frac{3}{2}$.) Since $\Omega = G^N$ for this situation, we may write $S = k_B \ln \Omega = N k_B \ln G$. If we compare this expression with the high temperature limit of equation (3.16), we see that the two give the same answer if $G = k_B T / h\nu$, the ratio of the two energy scales. This is a pleasingly plausible result. It means that the entropy of the oscillators is the same at high temperatures as that of a hypothetical equal-occupation system in which G states are occupied. As $k_B T$ rises, G continues to rise as higher levels (there are an infinite number in all!) come into play. Hence the $\ln T$ term. But the actual value of G depends on the ratio of $k_B T$ to $h\nu$. It involves the quantum energy-level scale of the oscillators, so that G and S are inevitably quantum properties.

3.2.3 Applications

1. *Vibrations of solids.* The assembly of identical harmonic oscillators was used by Einstein in the early days of quantum theory as a model for the thermal lattice vibrations of a simple atomic solid. He derived the result for the heat capacity (Fig. 3.10) as a universal function of (T/θ) with θ the so-called Einstein temperature characteristic of the solid. If we take a mole of solid, with N_A atoms, then, since each atom can vibrate in three dimensions, we should represent it by $N = 3N_A$ one-dimensional oscillators.

The Einstein model has good and bad points. The successes are:

(a) It gives the correct high-temperature (classical) limit, namely $C = N k_B = 3 N_A k_B$ per mole. From the view-point of the previous section, this success arises simply from the correct evaluation of the number of degrees of freedom of the solid.

(b) It gives the correct extreme quantum limit, namely $C = 0$ at $T = 0$, a mystery in classical physics.

(c) It is indeed found experimentally that the heat

capacity per mole is a universal function of (T/θ) for all simple solids, i.e. adjustment of a single parameter θ makes all results similar.

However, the bad news is that the form of equation (3.15) is grossly incorrect in the intermediate temperature regime. In particular the experimental lattice heat capacity is not frozen out so rapidly as the theory predicts at low temperatures, but rather is proportional to T^3 in crystalline solids. The reason for the poor showing of the Einstein model is that by no stretch of imagination does a solid consist of localized oscillators which are weakly coupled. If one atom of the solid is moved, a disturbance is rapidly transmitted to the whole solid; and in fact the key to a more correct treatment is to model the vibrations as a gas of ultra-high frequency *sound* waves (phonons) in the whole solid, a topic to which we return in Chapter 9.

2. *Vibrations of gas molecules.* The thermal vibrations of the molecules in a diatomic gas will be discussed in Chapter 7. In this case, rather unexpectedly, the Einstein model applies very well. Certainly the vibrations of one molecule are now weakly coupled from the vibrations of another molecule in a gas. However, our statistical treatment so far is appropriate to *localized* particles only, whereas gas molecules are certainly non-localized and in consequence indistinguishable. Not surprisingly, it is to a discussion of gases which we now turn.

Chapter 4
Gases: The density of states

In the last two chapters we have applied the statistical method as outlined in section 1.5 to an assembly of distinguishable (localized) particles. We now embark upon the application of the same method to gases. This involves two new ideas.

The first concerns the one-particle states (step I of section 1.5). A gas particle is confined to a large macroscopic box of volume V, whereas a localized particle is confined essentially to an atomic cell of volume (V/N). As a direct result, the energy levels of a gas particle will be extremely close together, with astronomical numbers of them being occupied at any reasonable temperature. This is in marked contrast with the localized case, in which the energy levels are comparatively far apart and the occupation of only a few need be considered. Actually it turns out that one can make a virtue of the necessity to consider very large numbers of states. This topic is the subject of the present chapter.

The second idea is how to deal with the indistinguishability of gas particles. This is vital to the counting of microstates (step III of section 1.5). The ideas are essentially quantum mechanical, explaining from our modern viewpoint why a correct microscopic treatment of gases was a matter of such controversy and difficulty in Boltzmann's day. The counting of microstates and the derivation of the thermal equilibrium distribution for a gas will be discussed in the following chapter.

4.1 Fitting waves into boxes

We are going to be able to discuss many types of gaseous assemblies in the next few chapters, from hydrogen gas to helium liquid, from conduction electrons to blackbody radiation. However, there is a welcome economy about the physics of such diverse systems. In each case the state of a gas particle can be discussed in terms of a wavefunction. And the basic properties of such wavefunctions are dominated by pure geometry only, as we will now explain.

Consider a particle in one of its possible states described by a wavefunction $\psi(x, y, z)$. The time-dependence of the wavefunction need not be explicitly included here, since in thermal physics we only need the stationary states (i.e. the normal modes or the eigenstates) of the particle. What do we know about such states when the particle is confined within an otherwise empty box of volume V? For convenience, let us assume that the box is a cube of side a (so $V = a^3$). Furthermore we assume that 'confined' means that must satisfy the boundary condition $\psi = 0$ over the surface of the box. Now we come to the 'economy' referred to above: we know that the wavefunction ψ is a simple sinusoidal oscillation inside the box. This simple statement is a correct summary of the solution of Schrödinger's equation for a particle of mass m, or of the wave equation for a sound or electromagnetic wave. Therefore the only way to achieve a possible wavefunction is to ensure that a precisely integral number of half-waves fit into the box in all three principal directions. Hence the title of this section! The problem is the three-dimensional analogue of the one-dimensional standing-wave normal modes of the vibrations of a string.

To be specific we choose the origin of co-ordinates to be at one corner of the box. The wavefunction is then given by a standing wave of the form:

$$\psi \sim \sin(n_1 \pi x/a) \cdot \sin(n_2 \pi y/a) \cdot \sin(n_3 \pi z/a) \qquad (4.1)$$

where the positive integers $n_{1,2,3}$ ($= 1, 2, 3, 4 \ldots$) simply give the number of half waves fitting into the cubical box (side a) in the x, y and z directions respectively. (The use of sine functions guarantees the vanishing of ψ on the three faces of the cube containing the origin; the internal values of the three ns ensures the vanishing of ψ on the other three faces.) Incidentally, in terms of our earlier notation the state specification by the three numbers (n_1, n_2, n_3) is entirely equivalent to the previous state label 'j'.

It is useful to write equation (4.1) in terms of the components of a 'wave vector' $\mathbf{k}$ as

$$\psi \sim \sin(k_x x) \cdot \sin(k_y y) \cdot \sin(k_z z) \qquad (4.2)$$

where

$$\mathbf{k} = (k_x, k_y, k_z) = (\pi/a)(n_1, n_2, n_3).$$

The possible states for the wave are specified by giving the three integers $n_{1,2,3}$, i.e. by specifying a particular point $\mathbf{k}$ in 'k-space'. This is a valuable geometrical idea. What it means is that all the possible 'k-states' can be represented (on a single picture) by a cubic array of points in the positive octant of k-space, the spacing being (π/a).

Now because of the macroscopic size a of the box, this spacing is very small in all realistic cases. Indeed we shall find later that in most gases the states are so numerous that our N particles are spread over even more than N states—most occupation numbers are 0. Under these conditions it is clear that we shall not wish to consider the states individually. That would be to specify the state of the assembly in far too much detail. Rather we shall choose to *group* the states, and to specify only the mean properties of each group. And the use of k-space gives an immediate way of doing the grouping (or graining as it is often called).

For instance let us suppose we wish to count the number of states in a group whose $\mathbf{k}$ lies with x-component between k_x and $k_x + \delta k_x$, with y-component between k_y and $k_y + \delta k_y$ and with z-component between k_z and $k_z + \delta k_z$. Call this number $g(k_x, k_y, k_z) \delta k_x \delta k_y \delta k_z$. Since the states are evenly spread in k-space with the spacing (π/a), the required number is:

$$g(k_x, k_y, k_z) \, \delta k_x \delta k_y \delta k_z = (a/\pi)^3 \delta k_x \delta k_y \delta k_z. \qquad (4.3)$$

The function g so defined is a 'density of states' in k. Its constant value simply sets out that the states are uniformly spread in k-space. However, this is a significant and useful idea. The number of states in any group can be evaluated from the volume in k-space occupied by the group, together with equation (4.3).

For example, to discuss the equilibrium properties of gases we shall make extensive use of another density of states function $g(k)$, which relates to the (scalar) magnitude of $\mathbf{k}$ only, irrespective of its direction. Its definition is that $g(k)\delta k$ is the number of k-states with values of (scalar) k between k and $k + \delta k$. Its form may be derived from equation (4.3) from an integration over angles. Since the density of states in $\mathbf{k}$ is constant, the answer is simply:

$$g(k)\,\delta k = (a/\pi)^3 \cdot \text{appropriate volume in } k\text{-space}$$

$$= (a/\pi)^3 \cdot (4\pi k^2 \delta k/8)$$

$$= V/(2\pi)^3 \cdot 4\pi k^2 \delta k. \tag{4.4}$$

In this derivation the factor $4\pi k^2 \delta k$ arises as the volume of a spherical shell of radius k and thickness δk. The $\frac{1}{8}$ factor comes since we only require the $\frac{1}{8}$ of the shell for which k_x, k_y and k_z are all positive (i.e. the positive octant).

Equation (4.4) is the most important result of this section. Before discussing how it is used in statistical physics, we may note several points.

1. The dependence on the box volume V in equation (4.4) is always correct. Our outline proof related to a cube of side a. However, the result is true for a box of any shape. It is easy to verify that it works for a cuboid–try it!–but it is not at all easy to do the mathematics for an arbitrary shape of box. However, a physicist knows that only the volume (and not the shape) of a container of gas is found to influence its bulk thermodynamic properties, so perhaps one should not be surprised at this result.

2. Rather more interestingly, the result (4.4) remains valid if we define differently what we mean by a box.

Above we adopted standing wave-boundary conditions, i.e. $\psi = 0$ at the box edge. However, this boundary condition is not always appropriate, just because it gives standing waves as its normal modes. In a realistic gas there is some scattering between particles, usually strong enough that the particles are scattered many times in a passage across the box. Therefore it is not always helpful to picture the particles 'rattling about' in a stationary standing-wave state. This is particularly true in discussing transport properties or flow properties of the gas. Rather one wishes a definition of a box which gives travelling waves for the normal modes, and this is achieved mathematically by adopting 'periodic boundary conditions' for a cuboidal box.

In this method, the periodic condition is that both ψ and its gradient should match up on opposite faces of the cube. (One way of picturing this is that if the whole of space were filled with identical boxes, the wavefunction would be smooth and would be exactly replicated in each box.) The normal modes are then travelling waves of the form:

$$\psi \sim \exp\left(ik_x x + ik_y y + ik_z z\right)$$

or $\quad \psi \sim \exp\left(i\mathbf{k} \cdot \mathbf{r}\right)$.

The values of $\mathbf{k}$ differ from the earlier ones in two respects, and indeed the microscopic picture is quite different in detail. The first difference is that the spacing of the k-values is doubled, since now the boundary condition requires fitting an integral number of full (and not half) waves into the box. Hence the spacing between allowed k-values becomes $(2\pi/a)$, and equation (4.3) is no longer valid—another factor of $(\frac{1}{8})$ is needed on the right-hand side. The second difference is that the restriction on $\mathbf{k}$ to the positive octant is lifted. A negative k-value gives a different travelling wave state from positive k; they represent states with the same wavelength but travelling in opposite directions.

This difference means that the integration between equations (4.3) and (4.4) should cover all eight octants of k-space. Therefore the two differences compensate for each other in working out $g(k)\delta k$ and the result (4.4) survives unchanged.

3. The next comment concerns graining. The states are not evenly spread in k-space on the finest level–they are discrete quantum states. Therefore we cannot in principle let the range δk in equation (4.4) tend to zero. The group of states we are considering must always be a large one for the concept of the (average) density of states to make sense. Nevertheless, in every practical case except one (the Bose–Einstein condensation to be discussed in Chapter 9) we shall find that the differences between adjacent groups can still be so minutely small, that calculus can be used, i.e. we can for computation replace the finite range δk by the infinitesimal dk.

4. The final comment is about dimensionality. Equation (4.4) is a three-dimensional result, based on the volume of a spherical shell of radius k. Entirely analogous results can be derived for particles constrained within one- or two-dimensional 'boxes'. For example the states of a particle constrained in two-dimensions to an area A have a density of states in k of:

$$g(k)\delta k = A/(2\pi)^2 \cdot 2\pi k\,\delta k.$$

The corresponding one-dimensional result for a line of length L is rather similar to equation (4.3) since no integration is needed:

$$g(k)\delta k = L/(2\pi)\delta k.$$

The reader might care to derive these results?

4.2 Other information for statistical physics

In the previous section we have described the geometry of fitting waves into boxes, a common feature for all types of gaseous particle. However, before we know enough about the states to proceed with statistical physics, there are two other ideas which need to be stirred in. Although the final answers will be different for different gases, the same two questions need to be asked in each particular case.

4.2.1 Quantum states are k-states plus

The first question relates to what constitutes a quantum state for a particle. The general answer is that the full state specification (labelled simply by j in earlier chapters) must include a complete statement of what can in principle be specified about the particle. The k-state of the particle (as given by the three numbers $n_{1,2,3}$ for our cubical box) is a full specification only of the translational motion of the centre of mass of the particle, as characterized by $\psi(x,y,z)$.

But usually there are other identifiable things one can say about the particle, besides its centre of mass motion. Firstly, one may need to consider internal motion of the particle, arising from vibration or rotation of a molecular particle for example. We shall return to this type of 'internal degree of freedom' in Chapter 7. Secondly, even for a simple particle, one must specify the spin of the particle, or the polarization of the corresponding wave, essentially the same idea. For example an electron with a particular spatial wavefunction and its spin up is in a *different* quantum state from an electron with the same spatial wavefunction but its spin down (hence the periodic table, for instance!). Similarly for an electromagnetic wave one needs to know not only its wave vector **k** but also its polarization (e.g. left- or right-handed).

The idea of spin may easily be included in equation (4.4). We redefine $g(k)\delta k$ to be the number of quantum states (and not merely k-states) with magnitude of k between k and $k + \delta k$. The equation then becomes:

$$g(k)\delta k = V/(2\pi)^3 \cdot 4\pi k^2 \delta k \cdot G \qquad (4.5)$$

where the new factor G is a polarization or spin factor, usually 1 or 2 or another small integer, dependent on the type of substance under consideration. In future all density of states functions like $g(k)$ will refer to quantum states and will include this spin factor.

4.2.2 The dispersion relation

The second vital idea is that to make any progress with statistical physics one must not only be able to count up the quantum states. One must also know their energies, ε_j in earlier notation. The point is simply that all equilibrium thermal properties are governed only by energy; the two constraints on an allowed distribution are those of energy and number.

In order to determine the energy ε_j, there are two considerations. The first of these is the 'plus' of the previous section. If there are internal spatial degrees of freedom, these will affect the energy (see Chapter 7). In addition sometimes the energy is spin-dependent, for example in the case of an electron in a magnetic field, and then this must be included and it will have important effects. But the second and more general consideration is that in every case the energy depends on k. We use $\varepsilon(k)$, or simply ε, in the rest of this chapter to represent the energy contribution from the translational motion, i.e. from the k-state. The $\varepsilon - k$ relation is often referred to as the dispersion relation. It contains precisely the same physical content as the $\omega - k$ dispersion relation in wave theory (since $\varepsilon = \hbar\omega$) and the $\varepsilon - p$ energy–momentum relation in particle mechanics (since $p = \hbar k$).

It is usually a convenience in statistical physics to combine the geometry of k-space (equation (4.5)) with the $\varepsilon - k$ relation to give a 'density of states in energy', often called simply the density of states. This quantity is defined so that $g(\varepsilon)\delta\varepsilon$ is the number of states with energies between ε and $\varepsilon + \delta\varepsilon$. It is derived from equation (4.5) by using the dispersion relation to transform both the k^2 factor and the range δk. This point is worth stressing. It is always worth writing a density of states function with its range explicitly shown, as for example on both sides of equations (4.3), (4.4) and (4.5). Although the same symbol g is used for $g(k)$ and for $g(\varepsilon)$, these two functions have different dimensions and units. It is the functions multiplied by their ranges, i.e. $g(k)\delta k$ and $g(\varepsilon)\delta\varepsilon$, which have the same dimensions–they are pure numbers. An example of this transformation is given in the next section.

4.3 An example–helium gas

As a specific example of the ideas of this chapter, let us consider helium (^{4}He) gas contained in a 10-cm cube at a temperature of 300 K.

The states are given by the solution of the time-independent Schrödinger equation for a particle of mass M in a field-free region:

$$(-\hbar^2/2M)\nabla^2\psi = \varepsilon\psi \tag{4.6}$$

with boundary conditions as discussed in section 4.1. The solutions are precisely those of equations (4.1) and (4.2). Substitution of these solutions back into equation (4.6) gives for the energies of the particle:

$$\varepsilon = \hbar^2 k^2/2M \tag{4.7}$$

i.e. $\quad \varepsilon = (h^2/8Ma^2)(n_1^2 + n_2^2 + n_3^2).$ $\tag{4.8}$

The energy $(h^2/8Ma^2) = \Delta\varepsilon_j$, say, gives a scale for the energy level spacing for a helium atom in the gas. It works out at 8×10^{-40} J, a very small energy compared with $k_B T$ which equals 4×10^{-21} J at 300 K. Clearly $k_B T \gg \Delta\varepsilon_j$, and from what we know already about energy scales this implies that a very large number of states will be energetically available for occupation in the thermal equilibrium state. Hence the whole approach of this chapter.

Finally we derive the density of states. Helium is a monatomic gas, so equation (4.5) gives the density of states in k. In this instance, since ^{4}He has zero spin, the factor $G = 1$. Hence $g(k)$ is known. The appropriate dispersion relation (from the Schrödinger equation) is equation (4.7), so the density of states in ε can be determined, treating k and therefore ε as continuous variables in view of the large numbers of states involved.

The calculation goes as follows. Starting from equation (4.7), $\varepsilon = \hbar^2 k^2 / 2M$, differentiation gives

$$\delta\varepsilon = \hbar^2 k \delta k / M$$

and inversion gives

$$k = (2M\varepsilon/\hbar)^{\frac{1}{2}}.$$

Equation (4.5) with $G = 1$ is

$$g(k)\,\delta k = V/(2\pi)^3 \cdot 4\pi k^2\,\delta k.$$

Substituting for k and for $k\delta k$ we obtain

$$g(\varepsilon)\delta\varepsilon = V/(2\pi)^3 \cdot 4\pi(2M\varepsilon/\hbar^2)^{\frac{1}{2}}(M\delta\varepsilon/\hbar^2)$$

$$= V2\pi(2M/h^2)^{\frac{3}{2}}\varepsilon^{\frac{1}{2}}\delta\varepsilon. \qquad (4.9)$$

This derivation nicely demonstrates the transformation from k to ε and the final result (4.9) will be a useful one in our later discussions of gases.

Chapter 5
Gases: The distributions

In this chapter the statistical method outlined in section 1.5 is used to derive the thermal equilibrium distribution for a gas. The results will be applied to a wide variety of physical situations in the next four chapters.

The method follows the usual four steps. Step I concerns the one-particle states. These were discussed in the previous chapter, and in fact no further specific discussion is called for until we come to particular applications. The one vital feature to recall here is that the states are very numerous. Hence we shall discuss gases in terms of a grouped distribution as explained in section 5.1. This discussion of possible distributions is step II of the argument. Step III involves counting microstates, i.e. quantum states for the N-particle assembly. In section 5.2 we briefly review the quantum mechanics of systems containing more than one identical particles. The counting of microstates is then outlined in section 5.3 and finally (step IV) we derive the thermal (most probable) distribution in section 5.4.

5.1 Distribution in groups

As discussed in the last chapter, the number of relevant one-particle states in a gas is enormous, often much greater than the number N of gas particles. Under such conditions, the definition of a distribution in states contains far too much detail for comfort. Instead we use effectively the distribution in levels, $\{n_i\}$ as defined in section 1.4.

The point is that it does no violence to the physics to *group* the states. In the form of the distribution used for computation the ith group is taken to contain g_i states of average energy ε_i. The only difference from the true specification of the states is that in the grouped distribution all g_i states are considered to have *the same* energy ε_i, rather than their correct individual values. This grouped distribution is illustrated in Fig. 5.1. Let us note several points before proceeding.

Fig. 5.1 Distribution in groups. The true distribution, containing very many states indeed, can be replaced by the grouped distribution for the purpose of calculation.

1. The grouping is one of convenience, not of necessity. We are choosing to use large numbers of states g_i taken together and also large numbers of particles n_i occupying these states. This will enable us below to use the mathematics of large numbers (e.g. Stirling's approximation) in discussing n_i and g_i in order to work out the distribution. But as physicists we can rest assured that more sophisticated approaches give the same mathematical results even if the groups are not assumed large (or if the grouping is not carried out at all); however, why not accept a short-cut if one is offered?

2. The grouping used in the distribution is arbitrary, but not capricious! The rule is that the number of states remains the same in both sides of Fig. 5.1. Or more precisely, the density of states (over a sufficiently course energy graining) remains unchanged. If we choose the energy levels ε_i, then the full microscopic

details of the true physical problem determine the values g_i.

3. A test for whether the grouping makes physical sense is to consider the average number of particles per state, often called the *distribution function* or colloquially the *filling factor*. This is defined as:

$$f_i = n_i/g_i.$$

Effectively, this filling factor f_i tells us the fractional occupation of a state of energy ε_i. In other words, within the density of states approximation, it can be thought of purely as a function $f(\varepsilon)$ of the energy ε. The test just referred to is a simple one. If the grouping has not violated the original problem, we expect that f_i will be a well-defined function of ε_i whose value does *not* depend on the details of the grouping. In particular, it should not depend on the value of g_i.

4. Finally, if we return to the example of helium gas (section 4.3), we can see that this approach makes some numerical sense. We noted previously that the energy level spacing between the true states ($\Delta\varepsilon_j$) was about 10^{-19} times $k_B T$. Therefore, it is quite possible to use groups of, say, 10^{10} states each (so that $g_i \gg 1$ in anybody's language), whilst maintaining an energy level spacing $\Delta\varepsilon_i$ which is still minute (about 10^{-9} to 1) compared to the thermal energy scale $k_B T$.

5.2 Identical particles–fermions and bosons

The next step (step III) in the statistical method is to count the number of microstates corresponding to a particular distribution. A microstate of course relates to a quantum state of all N particles, and here must come, therefore, the vital recognition that identical gas particles are fundamentally indistinguishable from each other. They are, therefore, effectively competing for the same one-particle states. We can never define *which* particle is in a particular state, the microstate is completely specified merely by stating *how many* particles are in each state. This counting problem will be tackled in the next section, but first there is another important question to be addressed. In quantum mechanics there are two different types of identical particle, which obey different rules as to how many particles can be allowed in each state. The particle types are called fermions and bosons.

Consider a system of just two identical indistinguishable particles. It is described in quantum mechanics by a two-particle wavefunction $\psi(1,2)$, in which the label 1 is used to represent all the co-ordinates (i.e. space and spin co-ordinates) of particle 1 and the label 2 represents the co-ordinates of the other particle. For $\psi(1,2)$ to be a valid wavefunction, two conditions must be satisfied. One is obviously that it should be a valid solution of Schrödinger's equation. But the second condition is that it should satisfy the correct symmetry requirement for interchange of the two labels. The symmetry required, that of 'interchange parity', can be outlined as follows.

If the labels of the two particles are interchanged, then any physical observable cannot change (since the particles are identical). This implies that

$$\psi(1,2) = \exp(i\delta)\,\psi(2,1)$$

since a physical observable always involves the product $\psi^*\psi$. The wavefunctions are related by the phase factor $\exp(i\delta)$. But if we make two interchanges, then we come to a mathematical identity, i.e.

$$\psi(1,2) = \exp(i\delta)\,\psi(2,1) = \exp(2i\delta)\,\psi(1,2).$$

Hence $\exp(2i\delta) = 1$, and therefore the interchange factor $\exp(i\delta)$ must equal $+1$ or -1, one of the two square roots of $+1$.

Particles which interchange coordinates with the $+1$ factor are called 'bosons', and those with the -1 factor are 'fermions'. We shall use the symbol S to describe the symmetric wavefunction of bosons, and A for the anti-symmetric function of fermions. It can be shown (not here!), or it can be taken as an experimental result, that all particles with integral spin (0, 1, 2, etc) are bosons; whereas odd-half integral spin particles (spin $\frac{1}{2}, \frac{3}{2}$, etc) are fermions. Therefore, for example, electrons and ^{3}He (both having spin $\frac{1}{2}$) are fermions; photons (spin 1) and ^{4}He (spin 0) are bosons.

Next, let us consider the case where the particles are weakly interacting, as is always the case in statistical physics. This means that a solution to Schrödinger's equation for the two particles can be written as the product of two one-particle wavefunctions, i.e.

$$\psi(1, 2) = \psi_a(1) \cdot \psi_b(2) \tag{5.1}$$

where the labels a and b are two values of the state label j for the one-particle states. However, as a wavefunction (5.1) suffers from the defect that it has no interchange parity, it is neither A nor S. Nevertheless it can be combined with its interchanged partner (an alternative solution to the Schrödinger equation with the same properties) to yield two wavefunctions, one S and one A. These are:

$$\psi_S(1,2) = (1/\sqrt{2}) [\psi_a(1) \psi_b(2) + \psi_a(2) \psi_b(1)] \tag{5.2}$$

$$\psi_A(1,2) = (1/\sqrt{2}) [\psi_a(1) \psi_b(2) - \psi_a(2) \psi_b(1)]. \tag{5.3}$$

The reader may readily check that these functions possess the correct parity, namely $\psi_S(1,2) = + \psi_S(2,1)$ and $\psi_A(1,2) = - \psi_A(2,1)$. The $(1/\sqrt{2})$ factors are for normalization purposes only.

Equations (5.2) and (5.3) bring out a fundamental difference between bosons and fermions. Consider the situation in which the labels a and b are identical, i.e. in which the two particles are both competing for the same state. For bosons, for which equation (5.2) applies, there is no problem. (In fact equation (5.2) gives an enhanced wavefunction compared to equation (5.1).) On the other hand fermions are quite different. The wavefunction given by equation (5.3) vanishes identically when we set $a = b$. This is the *Pauli exclusion principle*, which recognizes that 'no two identical fermions can occupy the same state'. I have heard bosons referred to as 'friendly particles' and fermions as 'unfriendly'. Although bosons enjoy multiple occupancy of states, in a fermion society all states are either unoccupied or singly occupied!

Finally we may readily generalize all the above results to an assembly containing N rather than merely two identical particles. The interchange argument is still valid between any pair of particles. Actually this makes it obvious that the choice of $+1$ or -1 must be a generic choice. When the first interchange considered is assigned a parity, an inconsistency will arise if all other interchanges are not given the same parity. All electrons are fermions, and all ^{4}He atoms are bosons.

For our assembly of N weakly interacting particles, the generalizations of equations (5.1), (5.2) and (5.3) are obvious but a little tedious to write down. Equation (5.1) becomes an extended product of N one-particle terms. For bosons, the expression for ψ_S is similar to equation (5.2), except that it contains $N!$ terms (every permutation of the particle co-ordinate labels) all combined with a $+$ sign. The normalization factor becomes $(1/\sqrt{N!})$. Similarly for fermions, the generalization of equation (5.3) is the one antisymmetric arrangement of the $N!$ terms; this will have systematically alternating signs, and may be written neatly as a determinant in which rows give the state label and columns the particle co-ordinate. But the vital feature is that the exclusion principle as stated above still operates—if there are two particles in the same state ψ_A is identically zero.

5.3 Counting microstates for gases

Now we are equipped to attack step III of the statistical method, that of counting up the number of microstates consistent with a given valid distribution. Since we postulate that all such microstates are equally probable, this step is the essential prerequisite to finding the most probable distribution, i.e. that which best describes thermal equilibrium, but that final step (step IV) follows in the next section.

The counting problem may be set up as follows. The

indistinguishable nature of the particles is accounted for by the inclusion of all permutations of the particle co-ordinates in the generalizations of equations (5.2) and (5.3). The microstate (effectively the appropriate wavefunction either ψ_S or ψ_A) can therefore be labelled just by the one-particle state labels a, b, etc. As pointed out earlier, this is simply a recognition that we cannot know which particles are in which states; even in principle we can only know which states are occupied. Therefore the counting of microstates is to specify the occupation of each one-particle state.

The distribution whose number of microstates is to be counted is the grouped distribution defined in section 5.1. The required number $t(\{n_i\})$ can be written as the product of contributions from each group of states, but the form of these factors will differ for bosons and fermions. The treatments of fermions (with the exclusion principle) and of bosons (without) are quite different in principle, which goes two-thirds of the way to explaining why this section has three sub-sections. The reason for the third will emerge below.

5.3.1 Fermions

As we have seen in section 5.2, the exclusion principle operates for fermions. Therefore, the one-particle states can only have occupation numbers of 0 or 1. Incidentally, this implies that in the ith group, the number of particles n_i cannot exceed the number of states g_i.

The counting is now straightforward. The group of g_i states are divisible into two subgroups: n_i of the states are to contain one particle, and therefore the other $(g_i - n_i)$ must be unoccupied. This is the 'binomial theorem' counting problem of Appendix 1, problem 2. The number of different ways the states can be so divided is

$$\frac{g_i!}{n_i!(g_i - n_i)!}.$$

This is the contribution to the number of microstates from the ith group. The total number of microstates corresponding to an allowable distribution $\{n_i\}$ is therefore given by:

$$t_{FD}(\{n_i\}) = \prod_i \frac{g_i!}{n_i!(g_i - n_i)!}. \tag{5.4}$$

The symbol FD is short for Fermi–Dirac, since these two physicists were responsible for the first discussion of the statistics of what we now call fermions.

5.3.2 Bosons

The statistics for bosons are called Bose–Einstein (BE) statistics, also named after their inventors. Counting the boson microstates is a little more tricky than for fermions since now any number of particles are allowed to occupy any one-particle state.

A direct, if slightly abstract, way of calculating the contribution from the ith group of the distribution is as follows. In the group there are g_i states containing n_i identical particles with no restrictions on occupation numbers. A typical microstate can be represented as in Fig. 5.2

Fig. 5.2 Counting bosons. In each group the g_i states are represented by $(g_i - 1)$ lines and the n_i particles by n_i crosses. In the illustration a microstate is represented for the case $g_i = 8$, $n_i = 9$.

by $(g_i - 1)$ lines and n_i crosses. The lines represent divisions between the g_i states, and the crosses represent an occupying particle. New microstates representing the same distribution, i.e. the same value of n_i for the group, can be obtained by shuffling the lines and crosses on the picture. In fact the contribution to the number of microstates is precisely a further simple binomial problem: how many ways can the $(n_i + g_i - 1)$ symbols be arranged into n_i crosses and $(g_i - 1)$ lines? The answer is the binomial coefficient (see again Appendix 1)

$$\frac{(n_i + g_i - 1)!}{n_i!(g_i - 1)!}.$$

This is the correct answer to the problem. But in fact, bearing in mind that in statistical physics we are always dealing with large numbers g_i of states, the -1 addition is negligible. It is adequate to use g_i rather than $(g_i - 1)$, and we shall do this forthwith. (Actually, if the -1 is retained here, then in the next section the mathematics would give a distribution n_i proportional to $(g_i - 1)$ rather than to g_i, violating the grouping requirement of section 5.1. The -1 would have then to be omitted for consistency, so we omit it from the outset!)

Hence our (slightly approximate) final result for the number of microstates to an allowed distribution for a boson gas is:

$$t_{\text{BE}}(\{n_i\}) = \prod_i \frac{(n_i + g_i)!}{n_i! g_i!}. \tag{5.5}$$

where again the product ranges over all groups i.

5.3.3 Dilute gases

For gases, there are two, and only two, possibilities. The gaseous particles are either bosons ($+1$, symmetric) or fermions (-1, antisymmetric). There is no half-way house. However, it is profitable to consider a third form of statistics quite explicitly, namely that of a dilute gas.

The word 'dilute' here has a specific meaning. It is to suppose that for all groups i, the states are very sparsely occupied, i.e.

$$n_i \ll g_i \qquad \text{for all } i.$$

We shall see later that this condition holds for real gases in the limit of low density and high temperature, and that it corresponds to a classical limit to either the FD or the BE form of quantum statistics.

In this dilute limit, we can readily see that both forms of statistics give almost the same answer for $t(\{n_i\})$. It is a result we should expect, since when $n_i \ll g_i$ even for bosons we would anticipate that almost all the states are unoccupied, and just a few have a single occupation. The existence or otherwise of the exclusion principle is irrelevant if the system is not even tempted towards multiple occupation!

To consider the fermion case first, each factor in equation (5.4) can be written as

$$[g_i(g_i - 1)(g_i - 2) \ldots (g_i - n_i + 1)]/n_i!$$

where both numerator and denominator have been divided by $(g_i - n_i)!$. Note that the numerator of this expression is the product of n_i factors, all of which in our present limit are almost equal to (but a bit less than) g_i. Therefore, we have:

$$t_{FD} \approx \prod_i \frac{g_i^{n_i}}{n_i!}.$$

In the boson case, equation (5.5) can be treated similarly in the dilute limit. Dividing top and bottom by $g_i!$ one obtains for the typical term:

$$[(g_i + 1)(g_i + 2) \ldots (g_i + n_i)]/n_i!.$$

Again the numerator is the product of n_i factors each approximately equal to (but a little larger than) g_i. Hence for the dilute boson gas:

$$t_{BE} \approx \prod_i \frac{g_i^{n_i}}{n_i!}.$$

Therefore in the dilute limit t_{FD} and t_{BE} tend to the same value, one from below and one from above. This 'classical' limit is called the Maxwell–Boltzmann (MB) case, discussed by these famous scientists before quantum mechanics was conceived. And we write the answer to our third counting problem as

$$t_{MB} \approx \prod_i \frac{g_i^{n_i}}{n_i!}. \tag{5.6}$$

5.4 The three distributions

It now remains to derive the three equilibrium distributions for the three counting methods of section 5.3. The techniques are precisely those set up in section 1.5 and already worked through for localized particles in Chapter 2. The aim is to find the most probable distribution consistent with the macrostate by maximizing the expression for $t(\{n_i\})$, just as in section 2.1.5.

5.4.1 Fermi–Dirac statistics

We require to maximize t_{FD}, or more conveniently $\ln t_{FD}$, subject to the usual macrostate conditions:

$$\sum_i n_i = N \tag{5.7}$$

and $\sum_i n_i \varepsilon_i = U$. $\tag{5.8}$

As before, the method is to simplify $\ln t$ using Stirling's approximation (Appendix 2), and then to find the conditional maximum using the Lagrange method. An outline derivation follows.

Taking logarithms of equation (5.4) gives:

$$\ln t_{FD} = \sum_i \{g_i \ln g_i - n_i \ln n_i - (g_i - n_i) \ln (g_i - n_i)\}.$$

The Lagrange method writes down for the maximum condition:

$$d(\ln t) + \alpha d(N) + \beta d(U) = 0. \tag{5.9}$$

Substituting $\ln t = \ln t_{FD}$ from above together with equations (5.7) and (5.8) for N and U gives after differentiation:

$$\sum_i \{\ln [(g_i - n_i)/n_i] + \alpha + \beta \varepsilon_i\} dn_i = 0.$$

The Lagrange method enables one to remove the summation sign for the specific, but as yet undetermined, values of the multipliers α and β to obtain for the most probable distribution:

$$\ln\left[(g_i - n_i{}^*)n_i{}^*\right] + \alpha + \beta\varepsilon_i = 0.$$

Rearranging this expression we find

$$n_i{}^* = g_i/[\exp(-\alpha - \beta\varepsilon_i) + 1].$$

As anticipated the grouping of the states has no explicit influence on the equilibrium occupation per state, and the result may be written in terms of a distribution function:

$$f_i = n_i{}^*/g_i = 1/[\exp(-\alpha - \beta\varepsilon_i) + 1]. \tag{5.10a}$$

The distribution function contains no detail about the states except their energies, and so in concord with the whole density of states approximation it can be thought of as effectively a continuous function of the one-particle energy ε_i or simply ε. Hence a useful form of (5.10a) is:

$$f_{\mathrm{FD}}(\varepsilon) = 1/[\exp(-\alpha - \beta\varepsilon) + 1]. \tag{5.10b}$$

This is the Fermi–Dirac distribution function.

5.4.2 Bose–Einstein statistics

The derivation of the Bose–Einstein distribution for a boson gas follows analogous lines.

Taking logarithms of equation (5.5) and using Stirling's approximation gives:

$$\ln t_{\mathrm{BE}} = \sum_i{}'\{(n_i + g_i)\ln(n_i + g_i) - n_i\ln n_i - g_i\ln g_i\}.$$

Substituting this into equation (5.9) together with the restrictions (5.7) and (5.8) gives:

$$\sum_i\{\ln[(n_i + g_i)/n_i] + \alpha + \beta\varepsilon_i\}\,\mathrm{d}n_i = 0.$$

The form of the equilibrium distribution is again obtained by setting each term of the sum equal to zero:

$$\ln[(n_i{}^* + g_i)/n_i{}^*] + \alpha + \beta\varepsilon_i = 0$$

which rearranges to give

$$n_i^* = g_i/[\exp(-\alpha - \beta\varepsilon_i) - 1].$$

In terms of the distribution function this becomes:

$$f_i = n_i^*/g_i = 1/[\exp(-\alpha - \beta\varepsilon_i) - 1] \tag{5.11a}$$

or $\quad f_{BE}(\varepsilon) = 1/[\exp(-\alpha - \beta\varepsilon) - 1] \tag{5.11b}$

the Bose–Einstein distribution.

5.4.3 Maxwell–Boltzmann statistics

For the dilute (fermion or boson) gas, the procedure may be followed for the third time, starting now with the expression (5.6) for the number t_{MB} of microstates.

We obtain

$$\ln t_{MB} = \sum_i \{n_i \ln g_i - n_i \ln n_i + n_i\}$$

which using equations (5.9) with (5.8) and (5.7) gives:

$$\sum_j \{\ln [g_i/n_i] + \alpha + \beta\varepsilon_i\} \, dn_i = 0.$$

Removing the summation for the equilibrium distribution and rearranging now gives:

$$n_i^* = g_i \exp(\alpha + \beta\varepsilon_i).$$

The final result for the Maxwell–Boltzmann distribution is therefore:

$$f_i = n_i^*/g_i = \exp(\alpha + \beta\varepsilon_i) \tag{5.12a}$$

or $\quad f_{MB}(\varepsilon) = \exp(\alpha + \beta\varepsilon). \tag{5.12b}$

One may note in passing that this distribution bears a marked similarity to the Boltzmann distribution for localized particles derived in Chapter 2. This greatly simplifies the discussion of dilute gases, since we have unknowingly already covered much of the ground, as we shall see in Chapter 6.

5.4.4 α and β revisited

After the lengthy discussion concerning α and β in Chapter 2, brevity is now in order. The parameter α again be related to the restriction (5.7) which spawned it. In the MB case this involves simply a normalizing constant. In the full FD and BE cases, the general idea is the same (α is adjusted until the distribution contains the correct number N of particles) but the mathematics is not so simple!

For the parameter β, the arguments of section 2.3.1 remain valid. They did not depend on the two assemblies in thermal contact having localized particles. Therefore β must be a common parameter between *any* two assemblies in thermal equilibrium, and following section 2.3.2 we continue to use the identity: $\beta = -1/k_B T$.

In summary, we have seen in this chapter that the distribution function, defined by the average number of particles per state of energy ε_i, is given for a gaseous assembly in thermal equilibrium at temperature T by the composite expression:

$$f_i = \cfrac{1}{B \exp\left(\varepsilon_i/k_B T\right) \begin{matrix} +1 & \text{(FD)} \\ 0 & \text{(MB)} \\ -1 & \text{(BE)}. \end{matrix}} \qquad (5.13)$$

In equations (5.13) the choice of $+1$, 0 or -1 is governed by which of the three types of statistics is relevant. The parameter B (equivalent to α since $B = \exp(-\alpha)$) is adjusted to give the correct number of gas particles. How the three distributions are used in practice will emerge from the following four chapters.

Chapter 6
Maxwell–Boltzmann gases

As a first application of the groundwork of the two previous chapters, we consider the simplest situation. This is a gas for which the Maxwell–Boltzmann (dilute) limit is valid. Furthermore we shall consider only monatomic gases in the present chapter, leaving the complications (and the interest!) of diatomic gases until Chapter 7. First we need to decide the practical range of validity of the MB limit. Next we can derive the MB distribution of speeds in the gas. Finally we may work out the thermodynamic properties of the gas and compare these to results from the ideal gas laws.

6.1   The validity of the Maxwell–Boltzmann limit

The MB distribution (equations (5.12) and (5.13)) may be written as

$$f_i = A \exp\left(- \varepsilon_i / k_B T\right) \tag{6.1}$$

with the constant $A = \exp(\alpha) = 1/B$. All of our discussion in this book applies only to perfect gases, in the sense of gases whose particles are weakly interacting. But in addition the MB distribution applies only to a gas sufficiently dilute that all the occupation numbers n_i are much less than the number of states g_i, i.e. that all $f_i \ll 1$. Taking the ground state energy as the energy zero (or close to it), the dilute condition therefore means that the constant A in equation (6.1) should be $\ll 1$.

Clearly in order to explore further we need to calculate A.

This is done using its associated condition (5.7):

$$N = \sum n_i$$
$$= \sum g_i f_i$$
$$= A \sum g_i \exp\left(-\varepsilon_i / k_B T\right)$$
$$= AZ \tag{6.2}$$

where the *partition function* Z is defined as the sum over all one-particle states of the Boltzmann factors $\exp\left(-\varepsilon_i / k_B T\right)$, just as in the Boltzmann statistics of localized particles (section 2.4). Hence the problems of calculating A and Z are identical. To make progress we now need the details of g_i, and that was the topic of Chapter 4.

To be specific, consider a monatomic, zero-spin gas such as ^{4}He. The states of a gas particle are then precisely those of 'fitting waves into boxes', equations (4.4) or (4.5) with $G = 1$. We have

$$g(k)\delta k = V/(2\pi)^3 \cdot 4\pi k^2 \delta k \tag{6.3}$$

as the number of states between k and $k + \delta k$, the wavevector k going from 0 to ∞.

Within the density of states approximation, the partition function is then calculated as an integral:

$$Z = \int_0^\infty V/(2\pi)^3 \cdot 4\pi k^2 \exp\left(-\varepsilon(k)/k_B T\right) dk. \tag{6.4}$$

The integral may be evaluated in (at least) two ways. One is to transform the density of states from k to energy ε, i.e. to evaluate

$$Z = \int_0^\infty g(\varepsilon) \exp\left(-\varepsilon/k_B T\right) d\varepsilon$$

with $g(\varepsilon)$ precisely that worked out in section 4.3 (equation (4.9)). The other entirely equivalent route is to use the dispersion relation $\varepsilon(k) = \hbar^2 k^2 / 2M$ (equation (4.7)) to transform the energy in equation (6.4), leaving a tractable integral over k. Using the latter method, we obtain:

$$Z = V/(2\pi)^3 \cdot 4\pi \int_0^\infty k^2 \exp(-bk^2)\,dk \qquad (6.5)$$

with $b = \hbar^2/(2Mk_BT) = h^2/(8\pi^2 Mk_BT)$. The integral in equation (6.5) is precisely equal to the standard integral I_2 discussed in Appendix 3, so that the expression becomes

$$\begin{aligned}
Z &= V/(2\pi)^3 \cdot 4\pi \cdot (I_2/I_0) \cdot I_0 \\
&= V/(2\pi)^3 \cdot 4\pi \cdot (1/2b) \cdot (\pi/4b)^{\frac{1}{2}} \\
&= V(2\pi Mk_BT/h^2)^{\frac{3}{2}}. \qquad (6.6)
\end{aligned}$$

Equation (6.6) is a central result for the MB gas, and we shall use it later in the chapter to calculate the thermodynamic functions of the gas. Meanwhile we return to the question of the validity of MB statistics. Having calculated Z, we have effectively calculated the constant $A = N/Z$ (equation (6.2)). For MB statistics to be valid we require $A \ll 1$.

It is worth putting in the numbers for the worst possible case! Consider ^{4}He at 1 atmosphere pressure and at a temperature of 5 K, at which it is still a gas (the boiling point is 4.2 K). Substituting the numbers (check it using the necessary constants from Appendix 4?) gives:

$$A = (N/V) \cdot (h^2/2\pi Mk_BT)^{\frac{3}{2}} \qquad (6.6a)$$

$$= 0.09$$

for this case.

This is a useful calculation. What it shows is that even for ^{4}He (and similarly for ^{3}He which boils at 3.2 K) the value of A is sufficiently small to justify the use of MB statistics as a first approximation (and as we see later in section 6.3, MB statistics lead to the perfect gas laws). A is often called the *degeneracy parameter*, $A \ll 1$ being the classical or 'non-degenerate' limit.

For helium gas near to its boiling point, the value $A = 0.09$ suggests that degeneracy will be a small but significant cause of deviation from the perfect gas laws. It is not too

straightforward to identify experimentally, since just above
the boiling point one unsurprisingly finds that corrections
due to non-ideality (interactions between atoms, finite size of
atoms) also cause significant deviations. However, the
degeneracy corrections are particularly interesting; since ^{4}He
is a boson and ^{3}He is a fermion, the deviations may be
expected to be of opposite signs. And so it is found.

For all other real chemical gases, and for helium at more
reasonable temperatures, the value of A is even smaller,
since the mass M and temperature T both enter as inverse
powers. For example, air at room temperature and pressure
has $A \approx 10^{-5}$. The nearest competitor to helium is hydrogen
gas, but this boils around 20 K. On the other hand, in the
free electron gas model of a metal, one uses an electron gas
at the metallic density. Here $A \gg 1$ since the mass is so
small, so that the gas is degenerate and FD statistics must be
used (see Chapter 8).

To conclude the section, let us note that A and Z are truly
quantum quantities. They depend on Planck's constant h,
and on the spin factor G ($= 1$ for ^{4}He). But when the
numbers are substituted, we find that the dilute MB limit is
entirely justified for real gases. Hence on that basis, the rest
of the chapter is worth the effort!

6.2 The Maxwell–Boltzmann distribution of speeds

Without really trying, we have in fact derived the distribution
of speeds of gas molecules in an ideal gas, the distribution
which plays an important part in the kinetic theory of gases.

In kinetic theory, one often requires the number of
molecules which have (scalar) velocities between v and
$v + \delta v$. This is given directly by the MB distribution–it is as
easy as $n_i = g_i \times f_i$. The number we require is conveniently
written as $n(v)\,\delta v$, defining the function $n(v)$ as a density of
particles in speed v. Hence we have

$$n(v)\,\delta v = g(v)\,\delta v \cdot A \exp\left(-\,\varepsilon(v)/k_B T\right) \qquad (6.7)$$

in which $g(v)\,\delta v$ is defined as the number of states in the
range of interest, i.e. with speeds between v and $v + \delta v$.

The number of states is obtained directly from the 'fitting waves into boxes' result, equation (6.3), with the simple linear transformation: momentum $= \hbar k = Mv$, i.e. $k = (M/\hbar)v$ (remembering that the range δk must be transformed to δv as well as the k^2 term to v^2!). The energy $\varepsilon(v)$ equals $Mv^2/2$; and the constant A is N/Z, with Z given by equation (6.6). Hence (6.7) is reduced to be a function of v only:

$$n(v)\delta v = Cv^2 \exp\left(-Mv^2/2k_\mathrm{B}T\right)\delta v \qquad (6.8)$$

with $C = 4\pi N (M/2\pi k_\mathrm{B}T)^{\frac{3}{2}}$. $\qquad (6.8a)$

This is the required result, obtained originally by Maxwell. It is an entirely classical result, as can be seen by the fact that h appears nowhere in it. In our derivation, the h^{-3} factor in Z (a detailed quantum idea, as discussed above) cancelled with an h^3 from the transformation from k to v. Another way of obtaining the constant C makes this point clear. If equation (6.8) is to describe the properties of N particles (gas molecules), then it must satisfy the normalization requirement

$$N = \sum n_i = \int_0^\infty n(v)\,\mathrm{d}v.$$

Integration of equation (6.8), having replaced the range δv by $\mathrm{d}v$, may be achieved using the integral I_2 (Appendix 3). It will be found that the value of C which satisfies this normalization condition is again given by equation (6.8a).

More comprehensive discussions of the properties and uses of the speed distribution are found in many books on kinetic theory. Some of its properties are illustrated in Fig. 6.1. The three different but representative speeds indicated on the graph are all of order $(k_\mathrm{B}T/M)^{\frac{1}{2}} = v_T$, say. They are as follows:

(i) v_{max} $(= \sqrt{2}v_T)$, the most probable speed corresponding to the maximum of the curve.

(ii) $\bar{v}$ $(= \sqrt{(8/\pi)}v_T)$, the mean speed of the molecules. This is again calculated using the integrals of Appendix 3 with $b = M/2k_\mathrm{B}T$. We write $\bar{v} = \int_0^\infty vn(v)\mathrm{d}v / \int_0^\infty n(v)\mathrm{d}v = I_3/I_2$, which gives the stated result.

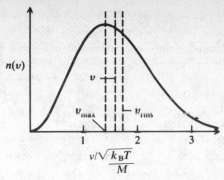

Fig. 6.1 The Maxwell–Boltzmann distribution of speeds in a gas. The representative speeds v_{max}, $\bar{v}$ and v_{rms} are defined in the text.

(iii) v_{rms} ($= \sqrt{3}v_T$), the root mean square speed. This is calculated similarly (albeit with even less difficulty since it involves the recurrence relation of Appendix 3 only) since the mean square speed $v_{rms}^2 = I_4/I_2$.

The evaluation of the mean square speed is of particular significance to the thermal properties, since it proves that the average (kinetic) energy per molecule is given by

$$\bar{\varepsilon} = Mv_{rms}^2/2 = 3k_BT/2. \tag{6.9}$$

Also since the gas is isotropic and has no net velocity the three component velocities must satisfy

$$Mv_x^2/2 = Mv_y^2/2 = Mv_z^2/2 = M(v_x^2 + v_y^2 + v_z^2)/6$$
$$= Mv_{rms}^2/6 = k_BT/2.$$

This is another example of the classical *law of equipartition of energy* referred to earlier in section 3.2. Each degree of freedom of the system, i.e. the translational motion of each molecule in each of the three dimensions of space, contributes $\frac{1}{2}k_BT$ to the internal energy of the system. We shall see this result again in the following section and in Chapter 7.

Finally, before leaving the topic, we may note that other more detailed statistical information can be compiled and used in a similar way. Again the key is $n_i = g_i \times f_i$, i.e.

number of particles in a group = number of states in the group × filling factor. Suppose for example one wants the number of particles with a velocity close to a particular value **v**. We may define the usual density functions for n and g such that $n(v_x, v_y, v_z)\,dv_x dv_y dv_z$ is the number of particles and $g(v_x, v_y, v_z)\,dv_x dv_y dv_z$ the number of states with velocity in the element $dv_x dv_y dv_z$ at velocity $\mathbf{v} = (v_x, v_y, v_z)$. Fitting waves into boxes in this case gives the g function to be a constant; the states are evenly spread in k-space, and hence in v-space also. And the Boltzmann factor in f_i is simply $\exp(-Mv^2/2k_BT)$ with $v^2 = v_x^2 + v_y^2 + v_z^2$. Therefore the result is

$$n(v_x, v_y, v_z)\,dv_x dv_y dv_z$$
$$= \text{const} \times \exp(-Mv^2/2k_BT)\,dv_x dv_y dv_z \qquad (6.10)$$

with the value of the normalization constant left as a problem (Appendix 5).

6.3 The connection to thermodynamics

This is an important section. We can now calculate the properties of a gas of weakly interacting spinless particles in the limit of low density. These are precisely the conditions for an ideal gas, one which obeys the equation of state $PV = RT$ with the temperature T being the thermodynamic temperature. We shall find the comforting result that our gas also obeys this equation of state, although our T was defined statistically from β. Hence we shall fully justify the statistical definitions of temperature and of entropy (see section 2.3).

The calculation methods for Boltzmann statistics can be used again here, so reference should be made back to section 2.5. The only caution is that the expressions for t^* are similar but not identical for the two cases. For localized particles equation (2.3) has a factor of $N!$, whereas the corresponding equation (5.6) for a gas of indistinguishable particles does not.

6.3.1 Internal energy and C_V

Since we have gone to the trouble of evaluating Z for a monatomic spinless gas (equation (6.6)), the quickest way to

U and C_V is to use Method 2 of section 2.5. The derivation of equation (2.27) depended only on the definition of Z, which is the same for gases as for localized particles. Hence

$$U = N\mathrm{d}(\ln Z)/\mathrm{d}\beta \qquad (2.27)$$
$$= Nk_B T^2 \, \mathrm{d}(\ln Z)/\mathrm{d}T \qquad (6.11)$$

using $\beta = -1/k_B T$. Since $Z \propto T^{\frac{3}{2}}$ (equation (6.6)), equation (6.11) at once gives

$$U = \tfrac{3}{2}Nk_B T. \qquad (6.12)$$

This is the result expected from the kinetic theory treatment of equation (6.9), since $U = N\bar{\varepsilon}$. The internal energy U for our perfect gas is a function of T only–it does not depend on V; and it is proved to have the value given by the old equipartition law. The expression for C_V follows at once:

$$C_V = \mathrm{d}U/\mathrm{d}T = \tfrac{3}{2}Nk_B. \qquad (6.13)$$

The heat capacity is a constant in the MB limit—a warning for lovers of the Third Law of thermodynamics that this limit cannot survive down to the absolute zero of temperature.

6.3.2 Entropy

To find the entropy, we use Method 1 of section 2.5, namely a direct evaluation of S from its statistical definition $S = k_B \ln \Omega$. For the MB gas, the calculation proceeds as follows:

$S/k_B = \ln \Omega$	definition
$= \ln t^*$	usual approximation
$= \ln \left(\prod g_i^{n_i}/n_i! \right)$	using t_{MB}, equation (5.6)
$= \sum (n_i \ln g_i - n_i \ln n_i + n_i)$	Stirling's approximation
$= \sum n_i (\ln g_i/n_i + 1)$	rearranging
$= \sum n_i (\ln Z - \ln N + \varepsilon_i/k_B T + 1)$	MB result for n_i/g_i, i.e. equation (6.1) with $A = N/Z$
$= N(\ln Z - \ln N + 1) + U/k_B T$	identifying U.

Hence the result for any MB gas (in this proof, no assumptions are made about any specific monatomic gas etc.) is

$$S = Nk_B (\ln Z - \ln N + 1) + U/T. \tag{6.14}$$

For the monatomic, spinless gas under particular consideration in this chapter, we have evaluated Z (equation (6.6)) and U (equation (6.12)). Hence in this case we have

$$S = Nk_B (\ln V - \ln N + \tfrac{3}{2}\ln T) + S_0 \tag{6.15a}$$

with the 'entropy constant' S_0 given by

$$S_0 = Nk_B [\tfrac{3}{2}\ln (2\pi Mk_B/h^2) + \tfrac{5}{2}]. \tag{6.15b}$$

Equation (6.15) (the Sackur–Tetrode equation) is an interesting result. It is classical in the sense that it cannot be correct down to the absolute zero; $\ln T \to -\infty$ whereas the physical S has a lower limit of zero at $T = 0$. Nevertheless it contains Planck's constant in the entropy constant S_0. Furthermore this constant can be checked by experiment. One measures the specific and the latent heats of a specific substance from essentially $T = 0$ up to a temperature at which the substance is an ideal gas. This enables one to calculate S calorimetrically using the fact that $S = 0$ at $T = 0$ from an expression of the type:

$$S_{cal} = \int_0 (C/T)\,dT + L_1/T_1 + L_2/T_2$$

the subscript 1 referring to the solid–liquid transition and 2 to the liquid–gas transition. In this way the value (6.15b) of the constant has been accurately verified.

6.3.3 Free energy and pressure

Now let us turn to the free energy F, and Method 3 of section 2.5, the 'royal route'. Without reference as yet to any specific gas, the hard work was done in the previous section in the derivation of equation (6.14). One can see that a very simple expression for F emerges, namely

$$F \equiv U - TS = - Nk_B T (\ln Z - \ln N + 1). \tag{6.16a}$$

Using Stirling's approximation in reverse, this may be neatly written

$$F = - Nk_\mathrm{B}T \ln Z + k_\mathrm{B}T \ln N!. \tag{6.16b}$$

The answer is the same as equation (2.28) for localized particles but with the addition of the $N!$ term. Our arguments from equation (6.16) branch along three rather distinct lines.

1. *Pressure*. First we can readily use $F(T, V, N)$ to calculate the pressure as follows:

   $P = - (\partial F/\partial V)_{T,N}$, since

   $\mathrm{d}F = - S\mathrm{d}T - P\mathrm{d}V + \mu\mathrm{d}N$. Hence

   $P = Nk_\mathrm{B}T(\partial \ln Z/\partial V)_{T,N}$

   using equation (6.16).

   For the monatomic MB ideal gas, since $Z \propto V$ (equation (6.6)), this becomes

   $$P = Nk_\mathrm{B}T/V. \tag{6.17}$$

   The result (6.17) remains true for polyatomic MB gases, since we shall see in Chapter 7 that $Z \propto V$ for these also; the box volume only enters Z via the translational motion of the molecules. Since this is identical to the ideal gas law, $PV = RT$, this justifies completely our statistical definitions of temperature and entropy. By calculating P and comparing with the ideal gas law we have verified:

   $$\beta = - 1/k_\mathrm{B}T \tag{2.20}$$

   and

   $$S = k_\mathrm{B} \ln \Omega \tag{1.5}$$

   with the constant $k_\mathrm{B} = R/N$, the gas constant per molecule, i.e. Boltzmann's constant.

2. *Extensivity*. Next, a few words about that extra $N!$ in equation (6.16b). For our treatments of gases or of localized particles to make sense, we require that the

extensivity is correct. If we double the amount of the substance, we expect functions like U, S and F also to double, so long as the doubling is done at constant T and at constant density N/V.

Now for a solid, the equation $F = -Nk_B T \ln Z$ (equation (2.23)) satisfies this requirement. The energy levels ε_j depend only on the specific volume, V/N. Hence $Z = \sum \exp(-\varepsilon_j/k_B T)$ is unchanged at given T and N/V. Therefore $F \propto N$ as required.

However, for a gas the extra $N!$ term is needed. Since all the gas particles are competing for the same space, we have $Z \propto V$, but independent of N (equation (6.6)). It is now Z/N which is unchanged when N is altered at constant density. Therefore equation (6.16): $F = -Nk_B T(\ln Z/N + 1)$ has the correct properties. The bracket remains unchanged and again $F \propto N$.

3. *The Gibbs paradox.* This was a classical problem of indistinguishability, perhaps a paradox no longer. Consider a box of fixed volume V and temperature T containing a mixture of two ideal gases A and B. We adopt a notation in which the subscript A refer to the properties which gas A would have in the *absence* of gas B; and similarly for subscript B. If the two gases are different then they behave independently, they occupy different states. Hence $\Omega = \Omega_A \times \Omega_B$, and $S = S_A + S_B$, $F = F_A + F_B$, $P = P_A + P_B$, etc. The two gases behave as if the other were not present. Even an isotropic mixture, say of ^{3}He and ^{4}He, behaves in this way.

However, the situation is different if the two gases A and B are identical. It is true that $P = 2P_A$, but $S \neq 2S_A$, and $F \neq 2F_A$. The molecules are now competing for states, so the statistical properties of the second gas are modified by the existence of the first. In fact we can see from equation (6.14) that $S = 2S_A - Nk_B \ln 2$ (arising from the $N \ln N$ term, i.e. from the $N!$) where N is the total number of A molecules. The degree of disorder is lessened by the competition.

Chapter 7
Diatomic gases

This chapter is a slight diversion, and could well be omitted at a first reading. However, the study of diatomic Maxwell–Boltzmann gases proves to be a rather interesting one. It will reinforce the ideas of energy scales, introduced in Chapter 2, and illustrate further the concept of degrees of freedom. Furthermore, the rotation of molecular hydrogen (H_2) gas holds a few quantum surprises. Throughout the chapter we shall assume, as is realistic, that MB statistics apply. The quantum surprises are not concerned with 'degeneracy', i.e. whether FD or BE corrections need be made to the statistics. But they are to do with the indistinguishability of the two H atoms which make up the H_2 molecule.

7.1 Energy contributions in diatomic gases

As outlined in the previous chapter, if the partition function of our MB gas is evaluated then all its thermal properties can be calculated. So far we have treated explicitly only a monatomic gas such as helium. What now about a polyatomic gas?

The problem is quite tractable, with one basic assumption. This is that the various forms of possessing energy are independent. To explain what this means, consider the contributions to the energy of a polyatomic gas molecule. The molecule can have energy due to translational motion, due to rotation, due to internal vibrations and (exceptionally) due to electronic excitation. If these energy contributions are independent, then it means, for example, that the state of vibration does not influence the possible energies of translation. In other words the one-particle states can be described simply as having energies:

$$\varepsilon = \varepsilon_{\text{trans}} + \varepsilon_{\text{rot}} + \varepsilon_{\text{vib}} + \varepsilon_{\text{elec}} \tag{7.1}$$

where each mode of possessing energy can be considered separately from the others.

This is an approximation only, but it is a good one. Translation, i.e. motion of the centre of mass, is accurately independent of the internal degrees of freedom of the molecule, i.e. motion around the centre of mass and excited electronic states. One might expect a small coupling between vibration and rotational states; for example, in a state of high rotational energy of a diatomic molecule the bond will stretch a little from the inertia of the atoms, and this will influence the bond strength and hence the vibrational frequency of the molecule. However, such effects are small in practice and may be (gratefully) neglected.

From the point of statistical physics, this independence has a great simplifying influence. It means that the partition function Z factorizes.

The partition function is defined (see equation (6.2)) as the sum over all states of the Boltzmann factors of every state. Writing β for $-1/k_B T$, and using equation (7.1) we obtain

$$Z = \sum_{\text{all states}} \exp\left[\beta(\varepsilon_{\text{trans}} + \varepsilon_{\text{rot}} + \varepsilon_{\text{vib}} + \varepsilon_{\text{elec}})\right]$$

$$= \sum_{\text{trans}} \exp\left[\beta(\varepsilon_{\text{trans}})\right] \times \sum_{\text{rot}} \exp\left[\beta(\varepsilon_{\text{rot}})\right]$$

$$\times \sum_{\text{vib}} \exp\left[\beta(\varepsilon_{\text{vib}})\right] \times \sum_{\text{elec}} \exp\left[\beta(\varepsilon_{\text{elec}})\right] \tag{7.2}$$

$$= Z_{\text{trans}} \times Z_{\text{rot}} \times Z_{\text{vib}} \times Z_{\text{elec}}. \tag{7.3}$$

The simplicity of equation (7.2) is that each full state of the molecule, by the assumption of independence, can be specified by its separate quantum numbers (i.e. state labels) for translation, rotation, vibration and electronic excitation. Hence the partition function factorizes as in equation (7.3) into independent component parts.

Since Z factorizes, $\ln Z$ has a number of additive terms. As a result there are independent additive terms in the thermodynamic functions such as F (equation (6.16)), U (equation (6.12)) and hence C_V. It is particularly instructive to note how this works out for the free energy F, since it becomes clear how to handle the $\ln N!$ term of equation (6.16b).

Substituting the form (7.3) for the diatomic gas into the general expression (6.16b) for any MB gas, we obtain

$$F = - N k_B T \ln Z + k_B T \ln N!$$

$$= - N k_B T \ln Z_{\text{trans}} + k_B T \ln N! - N k_B T \ln Z_{\text{rot}}$$

$$- N k_B T \ln Z_{\text{vib}} - N k_B T \ln Z_{\text{elec}} \qquad (7.4)$$

$$= F_{\text{trans}} + F_{\text{rot}} + F_{\text{vib}} + F_{\text{elec}}. \qquad (7.5)$$

The free energy of the gas is decomposed as anticipated into various parts. The translational part F_{trans} is defined by the first two terms of equation (7.4), which includes Z_{trans} together with the $\ln N!$ term. Note that this is identical to the total free energy of a gas of structureless (i.e. monatomic) molecules as worked out in Chapter 6. Hence F for the diatomic gas is equal to F for the monatomic gas *plus* additive contributions from the internal degrees of freedom, the final three terms of equation (7.4). The extra contribution of each internal degree of freedom is particularly simple. It gives merely a $- N k_B T \ln Z$ addition to F; and this is identical to the free energy of a set of *localized* particles (Chapter 2) with appropriate one-particle states. Therefore, we shall find that most of the hard groundwork for this chapter is already done, and that we may concentrate on the results.

7.2 Heat capacity of a diatomic gas

To be specific, let us use the ideas of the previous section to calculate the heat capacity C_V of a typical diatomic gas.

7.2.1 Translational contribution

As already indicated, this term holds nothing new above the content of Chapter 6. The translational motion of any molecule is described by the k-states of 'fitting waves into boxes' fame. And this treatment leads to a partition function (equation (6.6))

$$Z_{\text{trans}} = V(2\pi M k_B T/h^2)^{\frac{3}{2}} \tag{7.6}$$

with M being the mass of the molecule. Hence as before $U_{\text{trans}} = \frac{3}{2}Nk_B T$ and the heat capacity contribution is given by

$$C_{V,\text{trans}} = \frac{3}{2}Nk_B.$$

7.2.2 Electronic contribution

When we come to the internal contributions, equations (7.4) and (7.5) tell us that we can forget about the molecules being specifically those of a gas. Rather we treat the contributions as identical to those from an assembly of distinguishable particles.

Allowance for thermal excitation into a higher electronic state of energy ε above the ground state is identical to the treatment of the two-state system of section 3.1. The result in the heat capacity is to add to C_V a 'Schottky anomaly' term as given in equation (3.4) and Fig. 3.3.

In practice this contribution to C_V is negligible in almost all cases. This is because typical values of ε are around $10\,\text{eV}$, so that we are in the extreme quantum limit ($k_B T \ll \varepsilon$) at any realistic temperature. Hence $C_{V,\text{elec}} \approx 0$. The only exceptional everyday gases are NO and O_2. In these ε happens to be particularly small and the Schottky anomaly peaks are calculated to appear around 75 K for NO and 5000 K for O_2. However, with these exceptions it is justifiable to neglect the electronic term, and we shall do so in the rest of this chapter.

7.2.3 Vibrational contribution

Similarly, the contribution from vibrational motion has been calculated earlier in this book. Each diatomic molecule is accurately represented by a one-dimensional harmonic oscillator, and furthermore the molecules are very weakly interacting. Therefore, the vibrations of our N gas molecules can be described as an assembly of N identical and weakly interacting harmonic oscillators. This is the problem discussed fully in section 3.2. The heat capacity contribution $C_{V,\text{vib}}$ is given precisely by equation (3.15) and is illustrated in Fig. 3.10.

The heat capacity $C_{V,\text{vib}}$ is calculated to rise from zero to Nk_B as the temperature is raised, the change occurring around the scale temperature θ. As discussed in section 3.2, $k_B\theta$ is the energy level spacing of an oscillator, equal to $h\nu$ where ν is the classical frequency. Its value, therefore, will depend on the bond strength between the two atoms of the molecule and on their masses. For typical common gases θ turns out to have a value in the 2000–6000 K region (roughly 2000 K for O_2, 3000 K for N_2 and 6000 K for H_2 where the masses are lighter). At room temperature, therefore, vibration remains unexcited so that $C_{V,\text{vib}} \approx 0$ for all diatomic gases. At elevated temperatures the onset of vibration is seen, and the heat capacity rises. However, it often happens that, in practice, before $C_{V,\text{vib}}$ becomes very large the diatomic gas dissociates (into $2N$ monatomic gas molecules), the vibrational energy overcoming the bonding energy.

7.2.4 Rotational contribution

Having effectively disposed of electronic excitation and vibration, both theoretically and experimentally, we now turn to the rotational contribution. This will be found a more substantial topic!

The rotation of a linear molecule is modelled, bearing in mind the structures of section 7.1, by the motion of a rigid rotator. The rotator has a fixed moment of inertia I around an axis perpendicular to its own axis; spinning motion around its own axis is neglected. The solution for the quantum states of the rotator will be quoted here, but they should look familiar to a student who has studied any angular momentum problem in quantum mechanics. Basically the requirement for the wavefunction to be single valued upon a 2π rotation leads to quantization of an angular momentum component in units of $\hbar$. The allowed values of (angular momentum)^2 become $l(l+1)\hbar^2$, with $l = 0, 1, 2, \ldots$. And hence the allowed energy levels are given by:

$$\varepsilon_l = l(l+1)\hbar^2/2I$$

$$\equiv l(l+1)k_B\Phi \tag{7.7a}$$

where the temperature Φ so defined represents a characteristic temperature for rotation. These levels are degenerate, there being

$$g_l = (2l+1) \tag{7.7b}$$

states to level l, corresponding intuitively to different possible directions for the angular momentum.

Armed with these results we can at once write down the partition function for rotation:

$$Z_{rot} = \sum_{l=0,1\ldots} (2l+1) \exp\left[-l(l+1)\Phi/T\right] \tag{7.8}$$

Hence the problem is in principle solved, even if the sum (7.8) must be evaluated numerically rather than in terms of known functions.

Moreover, for all gases except hydrogen, there is a great simplification. When the numbers for the moments of inertia of a gas such as O_2 or N_2 are substituted into (7.7a), we find that the characteristic temperature Φ is about 2 K (2.1 K for O_2, 2.9 K for N_2 but 85 K for H_2). Since these gases have liquefied (indeed solidified) at such low temperatures, it is always true that $T \gg \Phi$. Very many rotational states are therefore excited, and the sum (7.8) may be replaced by an integral in this 'classical' limit. We write $y = l(l+1)$ and treat y as a continuous variable, so that $dy = (2l+1)dl$. Hence in this approximation:

$$Z_{rot} = \int_0^\infty \exp\left(-y\Phi/T\right)dy$$

$$= (-T/\Phi)\left[\exp\left(-y\Phi/T\right)\right]_0^\infty$$

$$= T/\Phi. \tag{7.9}$$

This simple result at once tells us the thermodynamic

properties of these diatomic gases. The thermal part of the total partition function Z (equation (7.3)) is obtained by multiplying Z_{trans} (equation (6.6)) by Z_{rot} (equation (7.9)). As discussed in Chapter 3, the ground state contributions from vibration and electronic excitation give rise to zero-point terms only. Since $Z \propto V$ (from the translational contribution only), it remains true that $PV = Nk_BT$ as discussed in section 6.3.3. But the additional factor of T in the partition function from rotation gives an additional Nk_B to C_V. And the total heat capacity is:

$$C_V = C_{V,\text{trans}} + C_{V,\text{rot}}$$

$$= (\tfrac{3}{2} + 1)Nk_B$$

$$= \tfrac{5}{2}Nk_B \tag{7.10}$$

a result which follows from $Z \propto T^{\frac{5}{2}}$, as the reader may verify (compare section 6.3.1). Hence also the ratio $C_P/C_V = \tfrac{7}{5}$ for the diatomic gas, a ratio in good agreement with experiment.

7.3 The heat capacity of hydrogen

As an example of the above results, we consider in greater detail the heat capacity of hydrogen. From what we have learned so far in this chapter, we anticipate the heat capacity of H_2 to resemble the sketch shown in Fig. 7.1. And in broad terms this is correct.

At temperatures just above the boiling point of H_2, the measured value of C_V is $\tfrac{3}{2}Nk_B$. At these temperatures, the molecules do not rotate! The moment of inertia of H_2 is so small that the $l = 1$ rotational state is further than k_BT above the ground $(l = 0)$ rotational state. In pictorial terms this means that the molecules remain in a fixed orientation as they move in the gas; collisions do not impart enough energy to start rotation. To return to the ideas of Chapter 3, the degree of freedom is frozen out since we are in the extreme quantum limit, i.e. $k_BT \ll \Delta\varepsilon$, where $\Delta\varepsilon$ is the energy level spacing.

Incidentally, we may note in passing that it is even more valid to neglect rotation in a monatomic gas (or axial rotation

Fig. 7.1 The variation of heat capacity C_V with temperature for a diatomic gas, showing schematically the contributions of translation, rotation and vibration.

in the diatomic case). Although the relevant moment of inertia is not zero, it is extremely small since most of the atomic mass is in the nucleus. Hence the first rotational excited state becomes unattainably high, and rotation is frozen out at all temperatures.

At low temperatures then, only the translational degrees of freedom of the gas are excited, and for the MB gas (equation (6.9)) each molecule contributes $\frac{3}{2}k_B T$ to the total energy from its translation in three dimensions.

By the time room temperature is reached, the rotational motion has become fully excited. Another way of looking at the problem is to note that the rotation of an axially symmetric molecule provides a further two degrees of freedom, two since two angles are needed to specify the direction of the molecule. And at room temperature the classical limit, $k_B T \gg \Delta \varepsilon$, is valid. Hence each molecule now contributes from its five degrees of freedom a total of $\frac{5}{2}k_B T$ to U, and therefore $C_V = \frac{5}{2}Nk_B$, in agreement with equation (7.10).

At room temperature vibration is in the extreme quantum limit ($k_B T \ll \Delta \varepsilon$) since the characteristic temperature of vibration (around 6000 K) is so high. However, at elevated temperatures, one expects the heat capacity to rise towards

$\frac{7}{2}Nk_B$ as vibration becomes excited. This is observed, although the gas dissociates before the classical limit is reached. (The detailed comparison with experiment is also complicated by significant coupling between vibrational and rotational states.)

7.3.1 The onset of rotation

Although the treatment so far gives a satisfactory outline of the properties of hydrogen, the details of the onset of rotation around 50–200 K are not well described. If we use the rotational partition function of equation (7.8) to calculate $C_{V,\text{rot}}$, we obtain curve A of Fig. 7.2. This is at variance with the experimental results for H_2, which are more like curve C.

Fig. 7.2 The rotational heat capacity of a diatomic gas. The three curves A, B and C are explained in the text.

Why the discrepancy? Actually an experimenter can help here. Nature is kind in that there are several sorts of 'hydrogen'. Using isotopic separation, it is possible to deduce C_V for the gases H_2, HD and D_2. Even allowing for the different values of Φ (H$_2$ 85 K, HD 64 K, D$_2$ 43 K) arising from the different moments of inertia, the curves for C_V differ markedly. And in fact our theoretical curve A is in good agreement with experiment for HD.

There is a great difference between a heteronuclear and a homonuclear molecule. It is a matter of the identity of the two nuclei. If the nuclei are different, and therefore distinguishable, then what we have done so far is correct. Hence the agreement for HD.

At first sight the modification to Z for identical nuclei might seem to be a simple one, merely to allow for the fact that a rotation of π rather than 2π leads to identity. However, the truth is more interesting than that, and the result is different for H_2 and for D_2. Let us concentrate upon the common gas H_2. The nuclei are just protons having spin $\frac{1}{2}$. The nuclei are thus identical fermions, and they must therefore be described by an *antisymmetric* wavefunction. In other words the wavefunction must change sign if the co-ordinates of the two protons are interchanged. The following discussion bears similarity to our earlier treatment of bosons and fermions in section 5.2.

The total wavefunction can be decomposed into the product of a 'space part' and a 'spin part'. The space part describes the rotation, and it is found that the $l = 0,2,4 \ldots$ states have even interchange parity whereas the $l = 1,3,\ldots$ states are odd. In the notation of Chapter 5, the even l states are S (even, symmetric) whereas the odd l states are A (odd, antisymmetric).

Consider first the even l rotational states. Since these are S, the only way to obtain a total wavefunction which is A is for the spin part to be A. And this means that the two spins must be opposite. There is just one such spin state corresponding to the total spin $S = 0$. Hence the even l rotational states must be associated with the spin singlet configuration only, and hence they have spin weighting 1. These states are often called 'para-hydrogen'.

On the other hand odd l states are A, the total wavefunction for H_2 is to be A, and therefore the associated spin part must now be S. This indicates the parallel spin states ($S = 1$), in which there are three possible alignments. Hence the odd l rotational states are linked with the spin triplet states, and they have a weighting of 3. The states are called 'ortho-hydrogen'.

The implication is clear. Assuming that our H_2 is in

thermal equilibrium, the partition function of equation (7.8) (although correct for HD) is in error. Rather than summing equally over the ortho- and para- states, we should have

$$Z_{rot} = \sum_{even} (2l+1) \exp\left[-l(l+1)\Phi/T\right]$$
$$+ 3\sum_{odd} (2l+1) \exp\left[-l(l+1)\Phi/T\right] \qquad (7.11)$$

where the even sum goes over $l = 0, 2, 4 \ldots$ and the odd sum over $l = 1, 3 \ldots$. When equation (7.11) is used to compute C_V, the result is curve B of Fig. 7.2, in even greater disagreement with experiment. However, the final twist to the story is uncovered when the experiment is done either very slowly, or better still in the presence of a catalyst such as activated charcoal. Then it is indeed found that curve B fits the experiment.

The reason for the poor fit to the experiment without the catalyst is that 'ortho–para conversion' is very slow. Changing l by ± 1 on collision requires a collision process which changes the total spin, and this implies the presence of a third body (i.e. a surface) to take away the spin. There is no such problem for collisions in which l changes by ± 2. Now the way the experiments are done in practice is to prepare and store the H_2 gas at room temperature, i.e. when $T \gg \Phi$. In this limit, the odd and even sums in equation (7.11) are equal (compare the discussion leading to equation (7.9)). Hence the ratio of ortho- to para-hydrogen molecules when the gas equilibrates at high temperature is $3:1$. When the hydrogen is then cooled, and experiments are performed with no ortho–para conversion, then the result is like a $3:1$ mixture of two dissimilar gases, and we find that

$$C_V = 0.75\, C_{V,ortho} + 0.25\, C_{V,para} \qquad (7.12)$$

where the ortho and para heat capacities are calculated respectively only from the odd and even terms of the partition function. This result gives curve C, at last in agreement with the usual experiment.

Two final points. Ortho–para conversion is a technical problem in H_2 in its use in refrigeration. If it is left to equilibrate at low temperatures, then much heat will be released as the $l=1$ states gradually relax to $l=0$. In addition all the thermal properties, even the boiling point, change with the ortho:para ratio. Hydrogen is best avoided in cryogenics! The second point is that similar effects occur in the gas D_2, although the details are quite different from H_2 since the deuteron is a boson (S wavefunction) rather than a fermion. We leave this topic as an exercise.

Chapter 8
Fermi–Dirac gases

We return now to the main stream of the book, and to the basic statistical properties of ideal gases as introduced in Chapter 5. Of the three types of statistics we have so far discussed only the classical limit, corresponding to Maxwell–Boltzmann gases. In the next two chapters so-called 'quantum statistics' are discussed, that is statistics where the antisymmetric (Fermi–Dirac) or the symmetric (Bose–Einstein) nature of the wavefunction plays a significant role.

The importance of the FD or BE nature is most readily seen when we consider the state of the gas at $T = 0$. At the other extreme, we have already noted that MB statistics are a high-temperature approximation, corresponding to the degeneracy parameter A (defined by equation (6.6a)) being $\ll 1$. As T approaches zero, and therefore A becomes infinitely large, the quantum limit is obvious. For BE statistics, in which any number of particles can occupy a state, the $T = 0$ state is for all N particles to occupy the ground state. This gives a situation of lowest energy and of zero entropy, i.e. of perfect order. In contrast to the 'friendly' bosons, the 'unfriendly' fermions operate an exclusion principle. Therefore the $T = 0$ state for FD statistics is with the N particles neatly and separately packed into the N states of lowest energy, giving a large zero-point energy, but again zero entropy (because of the lack of ambiguity in the arrangement).

In this chapter we now discuss the properties of FD ideal gases. The BE case is treated in Chapter 9.

8.1 Properties of an ideal Fermi–Dirac gas

As we have seen, FD statistics are needed, (i) when we are dealing with a gas of weakly interacting particles having spin $\frac{1}{2}$ (or $\frac{3}{2}$, $\frac{5}{2}$...), and (ii) when the gas has a degeneracy parameter $A > 1$. Since

$$A = (N/V)(h^2/2\pi Mk_BT)^{\frac{3}{2}} \qquad (8.1) \text{ and } (6.6a)$$

one finds in practice that FD statistics are needed only in a few cases of high density N/V, of low temperature T or of low mass M. Important applications are:

1. Conduction electrons in metals at all reasonable temperatures, and also in semiconductors with a high enough carrier density N/V.
2. Liquid ^{3}He at low temperatures.
3. Dense-matter problems in astrophysics, such as in neutron and white-dwarf stars.

Since each of these involves spin-$\frac{1}{2}$ particles, we shall explicitly consider spin-$\frac{1}{2}$ fermions only in this chapter. The generalization is straightforward.

8.1.1 The Fermi–Dirac distribution

The distribution function was derived in Chapter 5. The result (equations (5.10) and (5.13)) is usually written as:

$$f_{FD}(\varepsilon) = 1/\{\exp[(\varepsilon - \mu)/k_BT] + 1\}. \qquad (8.2)$$

The subscript FD will in future be omitted in the interests of clarity. In equation (8.2), we have made the identification of the 'Fermi energy', μ. This is simply another way of characterizing the parameters α (equation (5.10)) or B (equation (5.13)) as $B = \exp(-\alpha) = \exp(-\mu/k_BT)$. The symbol μ is appropriate since it turns out that this quantity is precisely the same as the chemical potential of the gas.

The form of equation (8.2) is shown in Fig. 8.1, where it is plotted at three different temperatures. It is not hard to understand. The distribution function $f(\varepsilon)$ is defined as the number of particles per state of energy ε in thermal equilibrium. Equation (8.2) bears the mark of the exclusion

Fig. 8.1 The Fermi–Dirac distribution function at three different temperatures. curve 1: $k_B T = 0.02 \mu$; curve 2: $k_B T = 0.1 \mu$; curve 3: $k_B T = 0.5 \mu$.

principle, since it guarantees that $f \leqslant 1$ from the $+1$ in the denominator. So curve 1 in the figure, corresponding to a low temperature, shows as expected that $f = 1$ for states with $\varepsilon < \mu$ but $f = 0$ for $\varepsilon > \mu$. There is a change-over region of energy width about $k_B T$ around μ in which f changes from 1 to 0. As T is raised somewhat (curve 2), this change-over region gets wider, although the extremes of the distribution are virtually unaltered. When T is raised further (curve 3) the whole form of the distribution is affected, tending towards the simple exponential MB distribution in the high T limit.

8.1.2 The Fermi energy

To use the FD distribution, equation (8.2) we need to know the Fermi energy μ. This parameter (being related to α) is fixed by the number condition $N = \sum n_i$, as explained in section 5.4.4. The value of μ will depend on the macrostate conditions (N, V, T), and in particular it will be a function of T. We start by calculating its value at $T = 0$. There are two obvious ways to proceed, and it is worth being aware of both of them.

Method 1. Use the density of states $g(\varepsilon)$. The definition and the form of $g(\varepsilon)$ should be well-known by this stage. The states are described by fitting waves into boxes, as in Chapter

4, to give the states in k. A transformation using the dispersion relation is then used to give the density of states in ε. The procedure is almost identical to that given in section 4.3 for helium gas, leading to the result (4.9). The only modifications to (4.9) are, (i) that the mass M should refer not to He but to the relevant particle mass, and (ii) that a spin factor $G = 2$ for the spin-$\frac{1}{2}$ fermions should multiply the result. Hence

$$g(\varepsilon)\,\delta\varepsilon = V4\pi(2M/h^2)^{\frac{3}{2}}\varepsilon^{\frac{1}{2}}\delta\varepsilon. \tag{8.3}$$

The determination of $\mu(0)$, the Fermi energy at $T = 0$, follows from the fixed number N of particles in the macrostate. In the density of states approximation we have (directly from the definitions of $g(\varepsilon)$ and of the filling factor $f(\varepsilon)$)

$$N = \int_0^\infty g(\varepsilon)f(\varepsilon)\,\mathrm{d}\varepsilon. \tag{8.4}$$

At the absolute zero, the Fermi function $f(\varepsilon)$ takes the simple form noted earlier, that $f = 1$ for $\varepsilon < \mu(0)$ but $f = 0$ for $\varepsilon > \mu(0)$. Hence equation (8.4) becomes

$$N = \int_0^{\mu(0)} g(\varepsilon)\,\mathrm{d}\varepsilon$$

which using equation (8.3) for $g(\varepsilon)$ may be immediately evaluated to give

$$\mu(0) = (\hbar^2/2M)\,(3\pi^2 N/V)^{\frac{2}{3}}. \tag{8.5}$$

Method 2. Someone who really understands the fitting waves into boxes ideas can use a pretty shortcut here. The states in k-space which are filled at $T = 0$ can be represented as in Fig. 8.2. The low energy states with energy less than $\mu(0)$ are all filled, and since $\varepsilon = \hbar^2 k^2/2M$ these filled states correspond to those with k less than some value (called the Fermi wavevector k_F) corresponding to $\mu(0)$. States with $k > k_F$ are unfilled. The sphere of radius k_F, representing the sharp boundary between filled and unfilled states, is called the Fermi surface.

Fig. 8.2 The Fermi surface. Illustrating the occupation of states in k-space at $T = 0$; the sphere has radius k_F ($* = $ occupied; $\circ = $ unoccupied).

The second approach to the determination of $\mu(0)$ is to recognize that this Fermi surface must contain just the correct number N of states. Hence we must have

$$N = V/(2\pi)^3 \times 4\pi k_F^3/3 \times 2 \tag{8.6}$$

where the first factor is the basic density of k-states in k-space, the second is the appropriate volume in k-space (that contained by the Fermi surface), and the final 2 is the spin factor for spin $\frac{1}{2}$. From equation (8.6) it follows that

$$k_F = (3\pi^2 N/V)^{\frac{1}{3}}$$

and therefore $\mu(0) = \hbar^2 k_F^2/2M$ is precisely as given above in equation (8.5).

Three remarks about the Fermi energy follow.

1. We can now quantify the need for FD statistics in the systems mentioned earlier, by substituting into equation (8.5). It is useful in so doing to calculate the 'Fermi temperature T_F', defined by:

$$\mu(0) = k_B T_F.$$

For example, if we are interested in electrons, equation

(8.5) can be written:

$$T_F = 4.1 \times 10^{-15} (N/V)^{\frac{2}{3}}.$$

For electrons at metallic densities (say 6×10^{23} electrons in a molar volume of $9 \times 10^{-6} \, \text{m}^3$) this gives a Fermi temperature of about 70 000 K. Therefore, at ambient temperatures we are always in the limit $T \ll T_F$, so that the system is dominated by FD statistics (see again Fig. 8.1). For electrons in a semiconductor, the Fermi temperature will be lower and there are some situations in which MB statistics are adequate. Finally we may note that the dense free electrons existing in a typical white-dwarf star have Fermi temperatures of around 10^9 to 10^{10} K. Since the internal temperature of such a star is (only!) a mere 10^7 K, this is again a highly degenerate fermion gas.

2. The calculation of $\mu(0)$ can be directly related to the degeneracy parameter A of equation (8.1). In fact substituting (8.5), together with the definition above of T_F, we obtain:

$$A = (8/3\sqrt{\pi})(T_F/T)^{\frac{3}{2}} \approx 1.50 \, (T_F/T)^{\frac{3}{2}}.$$

This result explicitly demonstrates that the degeneracy condition $A > 1$ is effectively equivalent to $T < T_F$. And correspondingly the classical limit $A \ll 1$ is the same as $T \gg T_F$.

3. There is a temperature variation to μ. In fact in the classical region μ diverges to minus infinity as $-T\ln T$, a result derivable from the methods of Chapter 6. However, in the degenerate region $(T \ll T_F)$ the variation is small, and can often be neglected. It is still determined by equation (8.4), the number restriction. The temperature enters only through the Fermi function $f(\varepsilon)$. But in the degenerate region (see again curves 1 and 2 of Fig. 8.1), the variation of $f(\varepsilon)$ is only a subtle blurring in an energy range of order $k_B T$ around μ. In fact if $g(\varepsilon)$ were a constant independent of ε, there would be virtually no variation of μ with T in the degenerate region. As T is raised, the filling of states

above the Fermi energy would be compensated by the emptying of those below. It is only when $g(\varepsilon)$ varies with ε that a small shift in μ occurs, to allow for the imbalance in numbers of states above and below μ. For a two-dimensional electron gas (exercise!), $g(\varepsilon)$ is a constant and $\mu(T) = \mu(0)$ to a high degree of accuracy. For the usual three-dimensional gas we have a rising function $g(\varepsilon) \propto \varepsilon^{\frac{1}{2}}$ and μ falls slightly. Using the results of Appendix 3 it can be shown that for this case:

$$\mu(T) = \mu(0)[1 - (\pi^2/12)(k_B T/\mu)^2 \ldots].$$

Since the variation is small, we shall in future not distinguish between μ and $\mu(0)$, unless confusion would arise. Note that the symbol ε_F for the Fermi energy will be used in place of μ in sections 8.2 and 8.3.

8.1.3 The thermodynamic functions

It remains to calculate the thermodynamic functions U, C_V, P and so on. We shall do this explicitly in the degenerate limit only, and shall sketch graphs to indicate how the functions connect to the classical MB limit. Numerical methods are needed to compute the shape of such graphs.

Internal energy U. The internal energy can be evaluated from the distribution function $f(\varepsilon)$, simply using the direct expression:

$$U = \sum_i n_i \varepsilon_i.$$

In the present context this becomes:

$$U = \int_0^\infty \varepsilon g(\varepsilon) f(\varepsilon)\, d\varepsilon. \tag{8.7}$$

At $T = 0$, $f(\varepsilon)$ is the simple step function, so that the integral is readily evaluated as:

$$U(0) = \int_0^\mu \varepsilon g(\varepsilon)\, d\varepsilon.$$

Substituting $g(\varepsilon) = C\varepsilon^{\frac{1}{2}}$ for the fermion gas, this gives:

$$U(0) = \left(\tfrac{2}{5}\right) C \mu^{\frac{5}{2}}$$

$$= \left(\tfrac{3}{5}\right) N \mu. \tag{8.8}$$

The result (8.8) follows without the need to remember C when it is recalled from the previous section that $N = \left(\tfrac{2}{3}\right) C \mu^{\frac{3}{2}}$ from the corresponding integral (8.4). This value of $U(0)$ represents a very large zero-point energy, an average of $0.6\,\mu$ per particle. It is a direct expression of the exclusion principle, that the particles are forced to occupy high energy states even at $T = 0$. (Fermions display tower-block mentality!)

Above $T = 0$, whilst yet in the degenerate limit $T \ll T_F$, the integral (8.7) can be evaluated using the method outlined in Appendix 3. The result is:

$$U = U(0) + U(\text{th})$$

$$= \left(\tfrac{3}{5}\right) N \mu + (\pi^2/6)(k_B T)^2 g(\mu) + \dots . \tag{8.9}$$

As expected, U remains dominated by the zero-point term $U(0)$, the second thermal term $U(\text{th})$ being small. This is a reasonable result. In hand-waving terms it follows from the subtle blurring of $f(\varepsilon)$ with rising T. At $T = 0$ we have seen that all states with energies below μ are full, whereas all those above are empty. At a low temperature T, from equation (8.2) or Fig. 8.1, it is evident that f changes from 1 to 0 over an energy span of order $k_B T$ around the Fermi energy, the occupation numbers of states outside this span being unchanged. Hence only a number of order $g(\mu) \times k_B T$ of the fermions have their energies changed, and the change in energy of these is of order $k_B T$. Therefore one would expect $U(\text{th}) \sim (k_B T)^2 g(\mu)$, as in equation (8.9).

Equation (8.9) is shown with the explicit factor $g(\mu)$, since this displays the correct physics, as just explained. It is precisely this 'density of states at the Fermi level' which enters many of the thermodynamic and the transport properties of a fermion gas. And equation (8.9) continues to give the right answer even when we are not talking about an ideal gas in three dimensions, and the density of states is not of the form (8.3).

Nevertheless, it is also interesting to return to the standard ideal gas. Substituting into equation (8.9) the appropriate density of states, equation (8.3), together with the expression (8.5) for the Fermi energy, we obtain for the thermal internal energy:

$$U(\text{th}) = (\pi^2/2)\, Nk_BT \times (k_BT/\mu). \tag{8.10}$$

This is a useful way of writing the ideal gas result. We see that the thermal energy (omitting a numerical factor) is essentially the MB result multiplied by the 'Fermi factor' (k_BT/μ). And this factor is (a) small and (b) temperature dependent.

Heat capacity C_V. The hard work is now done. The heat capacity C_V follows immediately, since

$$C_V = dU/dT$$

$$= dU(\text{th})/dT$$

$$= (\pi^2/3)\, k_B^2 T g(\mu) \tag{8.11}$$

in the degenerate limit, obtained by differentiating (8.9). Hence at low temperatures one has a linear, and small, heat capacity. For the ideal gas (as in equation (8.10)) its magnitude is again of order the classical value Nk_B multiplied by the Fermi factor (k_BT/μ). The restriction of thermal excitation enforced by the FD statistics ensures that the heat capacity is a small effect.

Pressure P. The pressure is also readily deduced from U. In fact it remains true that for a gas of massive particles $P = (\frac{2}{3})\, U/V$, independent of statistics. Hence PV and U are proportional. This relation follows from basic statistical ideas:

$$P = -(\partial U/\partial V)_S \qquad \text{basic thermodynamics}$$

$$= -(\partial U/\partial V)_{\{n_i\}\text{ fixed}} \qquad S \text{ depends on } \{n_i\} \text{ only}$$
$$= -\sum n_i(\partial \varepsilon_i/\partial V) \qquad \text{compare section 2.3.2–}$$
$$\qquad\qquad\qquad\qquad\qquad \text{only the energy levels}$$
$$\qquad\qquad\qquad\qquad\qquad \text{depend on } V$$
$$= (\frac{2}{3}) \sum n_i \varepsilon_i/V \qquad \text{see below}$$
$$= (\frac{2}{3})\, U/V. \qquad \text{as stated!}$$

The volume dependence of the energy levels depends on the dispersion relation alone. For our gas of particles of mass M, we know that $\varepsilon(k) \propto k^2$. But k, a dimension in k-space, is proportional to the reciprocal of the box size a, i.e. $k \propto V^{-\frac{1}{3}}$. Hence $\varepsilon \propto V^{-\frac{2}{3}}$. Each energy level depends on V in the same way, the $-\frac{2}{3}$ power law enabling one to replace $\partial\varepsilon/\partial V$ by $(-\frac{2}{3})\varepsilon/V$.

Therefore P follows the energy density U/V. The Fermi gas therefore is seen to exert a very large zero-point pressure $P(0) = (\frac{2}{3}) U(0)/V$. This plays an important role in considerations of stability in white-dwarf stars, where the pressure (of order 10^{17} atm) inhibits further collapse under the influence of gravitational forces. In the case of metals, electrostatic binding forces are large and the electrons are contained in the metal by the so-called work function of the metal, an energy which must be greater than μ for the electrons not to leak out.

Entropy S. The temperature dependence of S is readily obtained from C_V. We obtain a linear dependence on T (just as for C) in the degenerate region, S tending to zero as it should at the absolute zero. This passes towards the $\ln T$ variation in the classical region. A full calculation of S or of F is fairly complicated, and will not be attempted here. (There is no partition function Z to help on the way.) The best route is to use $S = k_B \ln \Omega$, together with the known form of $f(\varepsilon)$.

Figure 8.3 illustrates the schematic behaviour of the thermodynamic functions, U, P and C_V.

Fig. 8.3 The variation with temperature of the thermodynamic functions for an ideal FD gas. Note the low-temperature (quantum) and high-temperature (classical) limits. (a) Internal energy and pressure. (b) Heat capacity.

8.2 Application to metals

Since this is a major topic of any book on the physics of solids, this section will be brief. The free-electron model is surprisingly successful in describing both transport and equilibrium properties of the conduction electrons. The surprise is that the very large electrostatic interactions, both between pairs of electrons and also between an electron and the lattice ions, can for many purposes be neglected, or at any rate be treated as small. The outcome is that the conduction electrons can be modelled as an ideal FD gas, but the density of states is somewhat modified to take account of these interactions.

Thus the heat capacity of a metal has a contribution from the conduction electrons which is precisely of the form (8.11). Since T_F is so large (typically 70 000 K, as we have seen) this term is very small at room temperature compared with Nk_B. And the lattice contribution to the heat capacity of a solid (Chapters 3 and 9) is itself of order $3Nk_B$. Therefore, as a consequence of FD statistics, the heat capacity of a metal is very similar to that of a non-metal—a result confirmed by experiment. At low temperatures, the lattice contribution is frozen out as T^3 in a crystalline solid (Chapter 9). Hence the linear electronic term becomes readily measurable at around 1 K. Its magnitude is well understood from equation (8.11). A transition metal has a large density of states (the d-electron states) at the Fermi energy compared to a 'good' metal like copper. So the electronic heat capacity of copper is much smaller than that of, say, platinum.

The contribution to the magnetic susceptibility of the conduction electrons is also strongly influenced by FD statistics. In section 3.1.4 we discussed the magnetization of a spin-$\frac{1}{2}$ *solid* obeying Boltzmann statistics. In weak fields, the result was:

$$M = N\mu^2 B/k_B T. \qquad \text{(8.12) and (3.10)}$$

(In this section we revert to use of μ for magnetic moment; we shall use the alternative symbol ε_F for the Fermi energy.) When we come to consider the magnetic contribution from aligning the conduction electron spins in an applied field B, the situation is different. Most of the spins are unable to align because there are no available empty states.

Fig. 8.4 Calculating the magnetization of a spin-$\frac{1}{2}$ FD gas at $T = 0$. The left-hand half of the figure gives the density of states for spin down fermions, whereas the right-hand half is for spin up fermions. The full curve shows the densities of states when $B = 0$, the dashed curves when a field B is applied. Only a small number of the spins close to the Fermi energy (indicated by the shaded region) are able to realign when B is applied.

The problem is illustrated in Fig. 8.4, relevant to $T = 0$. The only spins which realign in the field are those in the shaded states, numbering $\mu B \times (\frac{1}{2}) g(\varepsilon_F)$, the factor of $\frac{1}{2}$ arising since only half the states are in the spin-down band. Each of these electrons has its spin reversed (i.e. changed by 2μ), giving a total magnetization of

$$M = \mu^2 B g(\varepsilon_F). \tag{8.13}$$

This expression is independent of T in the degenerate region, since the argument of Fig. 8.4 is unaffected by the blurring of the Fermi surface. Equation (8.13) is again a characteristic FD result. Since $g(\varepsilon_F) = 3N/2\varepsilon_F$ for the ideal gas, we see that the magnetization is reduced from the Boltzmann value (equation (8.12)) by the usual Fermi factor ($k_B T/\varepsilon_F$). Again the small magnitude and the lack of T-dependence of the magnetization are well confirmed by experiment, as is the dependence on $g(\varepsilon_F)$ in particular metals.

8.3 Application to helium-3

Helium-3 is a spin-$\frac{1}{2}$ atom, having a nuclear spin of $\frac{1}{2}$. Therefore ^{3}He gas is a fermion gas. However, as explained in Chapter 6, it never exists with a density high enough for FD statistics to be more than a small correction to the MB treatment. But that is not the end of the ^{3}He story, since it turns out that FD statistics can usefully be applied to *liquid* ^{3}He.

Again this idea should come as a surprise! There are very strong interactions between molecules in a liquid, and the atoms in liquid ^{3}He are no exception. One of the achievements of Landau was to develop the theory of a Fermi liquid, and to show that for many purposes it can be treated as a weakly interacting gas. However the particles of the gas are not ^{3}He atoms, but are ^{3}He 'quasiparticles', entities which can be visualized as bare ^{3}He atoms dressed with the interactions of other nearby atoms. After all, if one atom in the liquid is moved, then a whole lot of other atoms must move in order for the liquid to re-establish uniform density. The Landau model ends up with a gas with the same number N of particles as atoms, but with the *effective mass* of each particle being larger than the bare mass. In liquid ^{3}He this effective mass is about 3–6 times the atomic mass of ^{3}He, depending on the applied pressure and hence on the density.

This simple picture of liquid ^{3}He is well supported by the measured thermodynamic properties. The heat capacity follows the general shape of Fig. 8.3, in particular being linear at low temperatures. But the value of T_F deduced from experiment requires, as suggested by Landau, a large effective mass. Similarly the nuclear spin magnetization is found to follow the form suggested in section 8.2 for spin magnetization of a fermion gas.

These ideas also help to explain the highly unusual phase diagram of ^{3}He, shown in Fig. 8.5. There are two points worthy of note, both relevant to statistical physics. The first is that ^{3}He remains liquid, at modest pressures, right to the absolute zero. In this the helium isotopes are unique. The explanation is that the binding energy of the solid is so weak

Fig. 8.5 The phase diagram for ^{3}He (not drawn to scale).

that it can be overcome even by its zero-point vibrations, making the solid unstable until it is stiffened up by compression. This 'quantum manifestation' occurs in both ^{3}He and ^{4}He, showing that it has nothing to do with fermions or bosons. The second feature of interest occurs only in ^{3}He, namely the region of negative slope of the solid-liquid equilibrium line below 0.3 K. It is, therefore, specifically relevant to the fermion system.

An important result of thermodynamics is that such a slope can be related to entropy and volume changes using the *Clausius–Clapeyron equation* (see e.g. Finn section 9.4). This states that the slope of the equilibrium line

$$dP/dT = \Delta S / \Delta V$$

where ΔS and ΔV are, respectively, the entropy and the volume changes which occur when the phase change takes place. Usually when a substance melts, its volume increases (ΔV positive) and its entropy increases (ΔS positive). Therefore dP/dT is usually positive. A negative dP/dT can occur in two situations. Occasionally it happens that the solid contracts on melting, ice to water being the commonest example. In the case of ^{3}He, however, the volume change is normal. The peculiarity of ^{3}He arises entirely from an unusual entropy variation. Below 0.3 K the solid entropy is bigger than the liquid, in other words the solid is more disordered than the liquid!

This arises because the entropy of ^{3}He at these low temperatures is due principally to its spin disorder. In zero magnetic field, the spins in the solid behave precisely as a spin-$\frac{1}{2}$ solid, as discussed in section 3.1. They are totally disordered, giving an entropy of $Nk_B \ln 2$ at all temperatures above a few mK. The spins order by their own interactions at around 2 mK. The entropy is illustrated schematically in Fig. 8.6. On the other hand the Fermi factor keeps the liquid

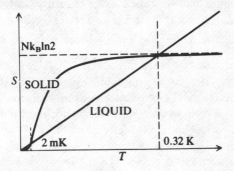

Fig. 8.6 Entropy–temperature curves for liquid and solid ^{3}He. In the anomalous (= unusual) region below 0.32 K the solid is more disordered than the liquid.

entropy low. As in our discussion of the heat capacity, only a small number (of order $k_B T g(\varepsilon_F)$) of the spins are free to change their state. The exclusion principle ensures that the others are frozen in, and at $T = 0$ zero entropy is achieved by all states below the Fermi level being definitely full and those above it being definitely empty: hence Fig. 8.6. The liquid (FD gas) entropy is not of course limited to $Nk_B \ln 2$, so that at a high enough temperature, it crosses the solid curve and continues upward.

Finally we can note that this phenomenon is more than a theorist's recreation. It forms the basis of 'Pomeranchuk cooling', a practical method for achieving temperatures as low as 2 mK. If liquid ^{3}He is precooled to a temperature somewhat below 0.3 K, and is then converted to solid by compression, refrigeration is produced. For instance if the conversion to solid were isothermal (T constant), Fig. 8.6 illustrates that a large amount of entropy would be extracted from the heat reservoir. On the other hand if the compression to form solid were adiabatic (S constant), the same $S-T$ diagram shows that the temperature of the ^{3}He would reduce. With reference to the phase diagram (Fig. 8.5), the liquid–solid mixture would pass up the anomalous (negative slope) co-existence curve as the pressure increases, until all the helium has solidified. The entropy scale on Fig. 8.6 is quite large, so that this is an effective cooling method.

Chapter 9
Bose–Einstein gases

This chapter discusses the properties of an ideal Bose–Einstein (BE) gas, which without any interactions nevertheless shows a remarkable phase transition, the 'Bose–Einstein condensation'. This property is relevant to liquid ^{4}He. But the principal application of BE statistics is to the 'phoney' boson gases, photons and phonons.

9.1 Properties of an ideal Bose–Einstein gas

9.1.1 The Bose–Einstein distribution

In Chapter 5 (equations (5.11) and (5.13)) we derived the form of the distribution function, i.e. the number of particles per state of energy ε in thermal equilibrium. For a gas of ideal bosons the distribution is

$$f_{\mathrm{BE}}(\varepsilon) = 1/[B \exp(\varepsilon/k_{\mathrm{B}}T) - 1]. \qquad (9.1)$$

For clarity the subscript BE will be omitted in the rest of this chapter. The parameter B is to be determined from the number conditions $\Sigma n_i = N$, which caused its appearance in the first place (see again Chapter 5). We shall discuss this number condition in terms of B for the boson gas, but it is entirely equivalent to the use of α or μ from the identities:

$$B = \exp(-\alpha) = \exp(-\mu/k_{\mathrm{B}}T).$$

Before coming to the determination of B, the main task of this section, we can observe some of its properties just from inspection of the distribution (9.1). To be specific, let us measure the one-particle energies ε using the ground state as the zero of energy, i.e. $\varepsilon_0 = 0$. Now to make physical sense, we know that for all ε the distribution $f(\varepsilon)$ must be positive. Because of the boson -1 in the denominator, this requires $B > 1$. If B were negative, then at least the ground state occupation would be negative! Furthermore, if one were to suppose $B = 1$, then the ground state occupation would be infinite, a possibility in a 'friendly' boson system since there is no exclusion principle. Hence we must have $B > 1$ to describe the finite number N of gas particles.

The value of B will be found to vary with density and temperature, as did μ in the discussion of FD statistics of α in the case of MB statistics. We can recognize from equation (9.1) that a simplification to the MB limit will occur when $B \gg 1$. Under these circumstances the -1 in the denominator will become insignificant for all values of ε, even for the ground state. Hence equation (9.1) could be replaced by the simple $f_{MB}(\varepsilon) = (1/B) \exp(-\varepsilon/k_B T)$.

The obvious approach to determining B, and the one used with success in the MB and FD cases, is to use the density of states approximation, and to replace the sum over all states by an integration over k or ε. So we enumerate the states by the usual function:

$$g(k)\,dk = V/(2\pi)^3 \cdot 4\pi k^2\,dk \cdot G. \qquad \text{(9.2) and (4.5)}$$

We shall for simplicity consider spin 0 bosons for which the spin factor $G = 1$. Making the substitution into equation (9.1) of $\varepsilon = \hbar^2 k^2/2M$, as is appropriate for a gas of particles of mass M, we obtain:

$$N = \sum_i n_i$$

$$= \sum_i g_i f_i$$

$$= \int_0^\infty g(k) f(k)\,dk$$

$$= V/(2\pi)^3 \cdot 4\pi \int_0^\infty k^2\,dk/[B \exp(\hbar^2 k^2/2Mk_B T) - 1]$$

or, after a little work,

$$N = Z \cdot F(B). \tag{9.3}$$

In equation (9.3) the factor Z is the same as the MB partition function for the gas (hence the notation), i.e. $Z = V(2\pi M k_B T/h^2)^{\frac{3}{2}}$. The function $F(B)$ is defined by what is left in the equation, which by the substitution $y^2 = \hbar^2 k^2 / 2Mk_B T$ is seen to be

$$F(B) = (4/\sqrt{\pi}) \int_0^\infty y^2 \, dy / [B \exp(y^2) - 1]. \tag{9.4}$$

Equation (9.3) can equally well be written as $F(B) = A$, where A is the usual degeneracy parameter (defined as N/Z). A is given by the (N, V, T) macrostate conditions, so that B can be determined from a table of values of $F(B)$ against B, a numerical task since equation (9.4) cannot be readily inverted. So is the problem solved?

To take the good news first, this solution certainly makes sense at high T or at low-density N/V, i.e. in the MB limit $A \ll 1$. In these circumstances, B is large, the -1 in the denominator of equation (9.4) is negligible, and the function $F(B)$ reduces simply to $1/B$. (This may be checked using the I_2 integral of Appendix 3.) This reproduces the correct MB normalization, $1/B = N/Z$ (Chapter 6). Furthermore, as A rises towards unity, nothing obvious goes wrong, and the above treatment gives plausible and calculable deviations from MB behaviour. However, as the gas becomes highly degenerate ($A > 1$), a nonsense appears, as we shall now demonstrate.

9.1.2 The Bose–Einstein condensation

If we lower the temperature far enough, then an apparent contradiction occurs. The difficulty is that, although we know that the minimum value possible for B is $B = 1$, the function $F(B)$ remains finite as $B \to 1$. In fact it takes the value $F(1) = 2.612\ldots$ Hence if $A > 2.612$, the equation (9.3) has no acceptable solution. This condition corresponds to $T < T_B$, where T_B, the Bose temperature, is defined by

$A(T_B) = 2.612$, i.e. by

$$T_B = (h^2/2Mk_B)(N/2.612V)^{\frac{2}{3}}.\qquad(9.5)$$

So, although our treatment makes sense when $T > T_B$, nevertheless when $T < T_B$ we apparently are not able to accommodate enough particles. The integral (9.3) is less than N even if $B = 1$.

The source of this difficulty lies in the total reliance on the density of states approximation. In particular, the approximation gives zero weight to the ground state at $k = 0$, which is effectively removed by the k^2 factor inside the integrand of equation (9.3). That is entirely valid if $g(k)$ and $f(k)$ are slowly varying functions of k. But we have already seen that in the region of $B \approx 1$, this is anything but the case. In fact $f(0)$ diverges as $B \to 1$.

A simplified (but essentially correct) solution to the problem is as follows. We group the states into two classes: (i) a ground-state group, consisting of the lowest few states—it makes no real difference exactly how many are taken. Assume g_0 such states at $\varepsilon = 0$, (ii) the remaining states of energy $\varepsilon > 0$. Since $f(\varepsilon)$ will be a smooth function over all $\varepsilon \neq 0$, this group may be described by the density of states approximation. Suppose that in thermal equilibrium there are n_0 bosons in the ground-state group, and $N(\text{th})$ in the higher states. Then the number condition (9.3) is replaced by:

$$N = n_0 + N(\text{th})\qquad(9.6)$$

in which the ground-state occupation is

$$n_0 = g_0/(B - 1)\qquad(9.7)$$

and in which the higher state occupations continue to be given by the same integral as in equation (9.3) (the lower limit of the integral is in principle changed from 0 to a small finite number, but this has no effect since, as noted above, the integrand vanishes at $k = 0$).

Equation (9.6) has radically different solutions above and below T_B. Above this temperature, the second term (corresponding to the vast majority of available states) can contain all the particles. We have $B > 1$ and hence $n_0 \approx 0$ from equation (9.7). Equation (9.6) becomes $N = N(\text{th})$, with $N(\text{th})$ given precisely by equation (9.3). Nothing has changed from the previous section.

Below T_B, however, the first term in equation (9.6) comes into play. We have $B \simeq 1$, so that the second term becomes $N(\text{th}) = Z \times 2.612 = N(T/T_B)^{\frac{3}{2}}$, using the definition (9.5). The first term is given by the difference between N and $N(\text{th})$, i.e.

$$n_0 = N[1 - (T/T_B)^{\frac{3}{2}}]. \tag{9.8}$$

This accommodation can be made with the merest perceptible change in B, B being of a magnitude $1 + O(1/N)$ throughout the low temperature region. Graphs of n_0 and of B are given in Figs. 9.1 and 9.2.

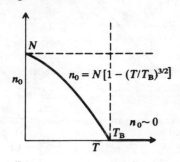

Fig. 9.1 The ground-state occupation n_0 for an ideal BE gas as a function of temperature. The ground state is not heavily occupied above the condensation temperature T_B, but below T_B it contains a significant fraction of the N bosons.

The properties of the 'condensate', the ground-state particles, are rather interesting. At $T = 0$, as expected, we have $n_0 = N$ and all the particles are in the ground state. However, even at any non-zero temperature below T_B we have a significant fraction (given by equation (9.7)) already dumped into the ground state. And these particles do not contribute to the internal energy, heat capacity, entropy, etc. The condensate fraction is already in its absolute-zero state.

Fig. 9.2 The variation with T of the normalization parameter B for an ideal BE gas. At and below T_B, B becomes hooked up at a value (just greater than) unity.

Fig. 9.3 The variation with temperature of the thermodynamic functions for an ideal BE gas. Compare Fig. 8.3 for the contrasting behaviour of an ideal FD gas. (a) Internal energy and pressure. (b) Heat capacity.

The thermodynamic functions obtained from the occupation of the states are illustrated in Figs. 9.3(a) and (b). The characteristic BE result for any function is:

(i) A simple power-law behaviour at $T < T_B$, arising from the $T^{\frac{3}{2}}$ dependence of $N(\text{th})$ together with the (effective) constancy of B. The variation of U is $T^{\frac{5}{2}}$, and so correspondingly is the variation of P (since $P = 2U/3V$ as shown in section 8.1.3). The heat capacity C_V varies at $T^{\frac{3}{2}}$ up to a maximum value of about $1.9\ Nk_B$ at T_B.

(ii) A phase transition at T_B, albeit a gentle one. In common parlance it is only a third-order transition, since the discontinuity is merely in dC/dT, a third-order derivative of the free energy; the second-order C and the first-order S are continuous.

(iii) A gradual tendency to the classical result when $T \gg T_B$, from the opposite side from the FD gas (compare Fig. 8.3).

Viewed from the perspective of high temperatures, the onset at T_B of the filling of the ground state is a sudden (and perhaps unexpected) phenomenon, like all phase transitions. It is referred to as the Bose–Einstein condensation. In entropy terms it is an ordering in k-space (i.e. in momentum space) rather than the usual type of phase transition to a solid, which is an ordering in real space.

9.2 Application to helium-4

The atom ^{4}He is a spin 0 boson. So just as we saw that FD statistics were relevant to ^{3}He, so we should expect BE statistics to apply to ^{4}He. Again, BE statistics are in the extreme only a small correction for ^{4}He gas, but their relevance is to the liquid.

Fig. 9.4 The phase diagram of ^{4}He.

Liquid ^{4}He remains fluid to the lowest temperatures at pressures below about 25 atm, for reasons discussed in section 8.3. Its phase diagram is sketched in Fig. 9.4. The outstanding feature is the existence of a liquid–liquid phase transition at around 2 K from an ordinary liquid (HeI) at high temperature to an extraordinary 'superfluid' phase (HeII) at low temperatures. The transition is evidenced by a heat capacity anomaly at the transition temperature, commonly called the lambda-point because of the resemblance of the C–T curve to the greek letter λ. The curve is shown in Fig. 9.5, with the corresponding S–T curve in Fig. 9.6. The nature of the singularity is 'logarithmic', in that although C_P is infinite, its integral across the transition is finite so there is no latent heat associated with the transition. The entropy curve is continuous, but it does have a vertical tangent at the transition. The low entropy of both liquid and solid (^{4}He has

Fig. 9.5 The heat capacity of liquid ^{4}He as a function of T, showing the lambda anomaly.

Fig. 9.6 The variation of entropy with temperature for liquid ^{4}He, showing a vertical tangent at T_λ.

zero spin!) below the lambda-point explains the very flat solid–liquid phase diagram in this region, bearing in mind the Clausius–Clapeyron equation.

All this bears some relation to the BE gas, although the actual transition in ^{4}He is more sudden than that of the ideal gas. It is believed that the difference can be attributed to the strong interactions between ^{4}He atoms in the liquid. Furthermore, the transition takes place at a temperature of the correct order of magnitude, the value of T_B for an ideal gas of bosons with the bare ^{4}He mass and the density of liquid ^{4}He being about 3.1 K.

Even more reminiscent of the BE gas is the nature of the superfluid HeII. Its properties are well described by a 'two-fluid model', in which the liquid is thought of as a mixture of two interpenetrating fluids. One of these, the normal fluid, has the properties of a conventional fluid, very like the thermal N(th) fraction of the BE gas (equation (9.6)). Whereas the other fluid, the superfluid, behaves like the condensate fraction n_0, in that it carries no entropy and displays no friction.

An excellent example of the properties arises when the viscosity of liquid HeII is measured. The answer is found to depend dramatically on the type of experimental method.

  (i) If viscosity is measured by the drag on a rotating disc or a vibrating wire, then a reasonable value is found, similar to that for HeI, although reducing somewhat as T is lowered well below T_λ.

 (ii) If, however, the measurement is made by allowing the helium to flow through tubes, one finds the astonishing answer zero for the viscosity. The fluid can flow with alarming ease (up to some critical velocity) through the thinnest channels; hence the term 'superfluid'. It can even syphon itself over the edge of a container through superflow in the surface film.

The explanation in terms of the two fluids is clear. The drag methods will pick out the most viscous fluid, and that is the normal fluid. The gradual reduction below T_λ arises from the gradual reduction of the normal fluid concentration (cf. $N(\text{th})$) as T is lowered. On the other hand the flow experiments pick out the smallest viscosity. Only the superfluid flows through a fine tube, and this has zero viscosity since it carries no entropy. A demonstration that it is the (effectively $T = 0$) superfluid only which flows is to observe that the flow produces a temperature difference between the ends of the flow tube. The source reservoir warms up as it is depleted of superfluid whereas the receiving reservoir cools down as the superfluid enters.

9.3 Phoney bosons

A boson is a particle of spin $0, 1, 2, \ldots$ by definition. Our discussion so far in the chapter has been based on an ideal gas of 'real' particles of mass M. However, there is another case, which is that the bosons could be particles with no rest mass. The obvious example is a photon gas. An evacuated box is never 'empty', in that it will contain electromagnetic radiation in thermal equilibrium with the walls of the box. Such thermal equilibrium radiation is called black-body radiation, and it may best be considered as a BE gas, an ideal gas of photons. The second analogous example is that the lattice vibrations of a solid can be modelled similarly as a gas of sound waves, or 'phonons', in a box which is the boundary of the solid.

The new feature of both of these gases is that the particles of the gas are massless. This has the importance that the *number* of the gas particles is not fixed. The particles may be, and are, destroyed and created continually. There is no conservation of N in the macrostate and the system is defined not by (N, V, T) but simply by (V, T). The empty box will come to equilibrium with a certain average number and energy of photons (or phonons) which are dependent only on the temperature and the volume of the box. So when we derive the thermal equilibrium distribution for the gas, there is a change. The usual number restriction $\sum n_i = N$ (equation (5.7)) does not enter, and the derivation of the distribution (section 5.4.2) is to be followed through without it. The answer is almost self-evident. Since there is no N restriction, there is no α (so also no B, and no chemical potential μ). But the rest of the derivation is as before, and we obtain the 'modified BE' distribution:

$$f(\varepsilon) = 1/[\exp(-\beta\varepsilon) - 1] \tag{9.9}$$

with as usual $\beta = -1/k_B T$. We shall now apply this result to photons and phonons.

9.3.1 Photons and black-body radiation

This is an important topic. The radiation may be characterized by its 'spectral density', $u(\nu)$, defined such that $u(\nu)\,\delta\nu$ is the energy of the radiation with frequencies between ν and $\nu + \delta\nu$. This spectral density was studied experimentally and theoretically in the last century and was the spur for Planck in the early 1900s to first postulate quantization, an idea then taken up by Einstein. The Planck radiation law, of great historical and practical importance, can be readily derived using the ideas of this chapter, as we shall now see.

The modified BE distribution (equation (9.9)) tells us the number of photons per state of energy ε in thermal equilibrium at temperature T. In order to calculate the spectral density, we also need to know, (i) how many states there are in the frequency range of interest, and (ii) how the frequency ν of a photon relates to its energy ε. The second question is immediately answered by $\varepsilon = h\nu$. The first is yet another straightforward example of fitting waves into boxes.

The density of photon states in k is given by equation (4.5), with the polarization factor $G = 2$. Photons, since they are spin 1, massless bosons, have two polarization states; in classical terms electromagnetic waves are transverse, giving left- or right-hand polarizations, but there is no longitudinal wave. Hence

$$g(k)\,\delta k = V/(2\pi)^3 \cdot 4\pi k^2\,\delta k \cdot 2. \tag{9.10}$$

We wish to translate equation (9.10) to a density of states in frequency ν, corresponding to the required spectral energy density. This is readily and accurately achieved for photons in vacuum, since $\nu = ck/2\pi$, where c is the speed of light. Making the change of variables, equation (9.10) becomes:

$$g(\nu)\,\delta\nu = V \cdot 8\pi\nu^2\,\delta\nu/c^3. \tag{9.11}$$

The answer now follows at once. The energy in a range is the number of states in that range × the number of photons per state × the energy per photon. That is:

$$
\begin{aligned}
u(\nu)\,\delta\nu &= g(\nu)\,\delta\nu \times f(\nu) \times \varepsilon(\nu) \\
&= V \cdot 8\pi\nu^2\,\delta\nu/c^3 \times \\
&\quad 1/[\exp(h\nu/k_B T) - 1] \times h\nu \\
&= V \cdot \frac{8\pi h\nu^3\delta\nu}{c^3} \cdot \frac{1}{[\exp(h\nu/k_B T) - 1]}
\end{aligned} \tag{9.12}
$$

Equation (9.12) is the celebrated Planck radiation formula. It is drawn in Fig. 9.7 for three different temperatures. We can make several comments.

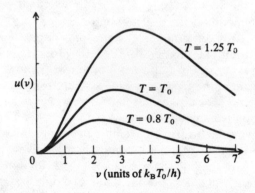

Fig. 9.7 The spectral distribution of energy in black-body radiation. The Planck formula (equation (9.12)) for the energy density as a function of frequency is shown at three different temperatures.

1. This is not how Planck derived it! Photons had not been invented in 1900. His argument was based on a localized oscillator model, in which each of the $g(\nu)\delta\nu$ oscillator modes had an average thermal

energy *not* of k_BT, the classical incorrect result, but of $h\nu/[\exp(h\nu/k_BT)-1]$ as derived in Chapter 3 (essentially equation (3.13) ignoring zero-point energy). The modern derivation is much to be preferred.

2. The Planck law is in excellent agreement with experiment. One of the features concerns the maximum in $u(\nu)$. Experiment (effectively Wien's law) shows that ν_{max} is proportional to T. This is evident from equation (9.12), since the maximum will occur at a fixed value of the dimensionless variable $y = h\nu/k_BT$. In fact y_{max} is a little less than 3 (see the problems in Appendix 5).

3. Another experimental property is that the total energy in the radiation is proportional to T^4. This T^4 law follows from an integration of the Planck law (9.12) over all possible frequencies. We have for the (internal) energy per unit volume:

$$U/V = (8\pi h/c^3)\int_0^\infty \nu^3\,d\nu/[\exp(h\nu/k_BT)-1]$$

$$= (8\pi h/c^3)(k_BT/h)^4\int_0^\infty y^3\,dy/[\exp(y)-1]. \quad (9.13)$$

The definite integral in equation (9.13) has the ('well-known') value of $\pi^4/15$. The energy U is represented by the area under the curves in Fig. 9.7, which displays the rapid variation of U and T.

4. Once U/V is known, two other properties follow. One is the energy flux radiated from a black body, a very accessible experimental quantity. It is defined as the energy per second leaving a small hole of unit area in the wall of the box, assuming no inward flux. (If the temperatures of the box and of its surroundings are the same, then of course there will be no *net* flux – usually a difference between flux in and flux out is the directly measurable quantity.) Since all the photons are moving with the same speed c, the number crossing unit area in unit time is $(\frac{1}{4})(N/V)c$, where N/V is the (average) number density of photons. The factor $(\frac{1}{4})$ comes from

the appropriate angular integration, as in the corresponding standard problem in gas kinetic theory. Hence the energy crossing unit area in unit time is $(\frac{1}{4})(U/V)c \equiv \sigma T^4$. This result is the Stefan–Boltzmann law, and the value of σ deduced from equation (9.13) is in excellent agreement with experiment.

5. The second property is the pressure, the 'radiation pressure'. We have already seen (section 8.1.3) that for a gas of massive particles, $PV = 2U/3$, this relationship following from the dispersion relation $\varepsilon \propto k^2 \propto V^{-\frac{2}{3}}$. For the photon gas, the dispersion relation is different, namely $\varepsilon = h\nu = ck/2\pi$. Hence $\varepsilon \propto k \propto V^{-\frac{1}{3}}$ in this case, and therefore (following the argument of 8.1.3) $P = U/3V$. The radiation pressure is simply one-third of the energy per unit volume.

6. Finally let us consider the range of validity of the T^4 law. No high-temperature limit is evident, since photon states exist well above the highest conceivable thermally excited frequencies. No problem exists here (unlike the phonon case discussed below). At low temperatures, however, we should see the breakdown of the density of states approximation. The T^4 law is based on the replacement of a sum over photon states by an integral over a smooth density of states. This will clearly become invalid in a box of linear dimension a when $k_B T < \Delta \varepsilon$, the energy level spacing, i.e. for $k_B T < ch/a$. This corresponds roughly to $T < 1$ K for a box of side 1 cm, but $T = 1$ K is just too low a temperature for radiation to be important in practice anyway.

9.3.2 Phonons and lattice vibrations

The same ideas may be applied to a discussion of the thermal lattice vibrations of a simple atomic solid. We have already noted in Chapter 3 the inappropriateness of the localized oscillator model, since the motion of one atom in the solid is strongly coupled to that of another. The weakly coupled vibrational modes are sound waves, and hence it is appealing to consider the vibrations of the lump of solid as the motion of a gas of sound waves in a box. Hence the similarity to the previous section, where a box of electromagnetic waves was discussed.

The weakly interacting gas particles, quantized sound waves, are called phonons. And the total internal energy U of the phonon gas can be calculated in an analogous way to equation (9.13). However, there are three important differences in comparison with the photon gas:

1. Sound waves have $G = 3$, not $G = 2$. The three polarizations arise from three-dimensional motion of the atoms in the solid. In the long wavelength limit, there are two transverse polarization modes and one longitudinal mode. Hence equation (9.13) should be multiplied by a factor 3/2.

2. The dispersion relation is altered. To a first approximation we can simply use $\varepsilon = h\nu = c_S k/2\pi$, where c_S is a suitable average velocity of sound. This will simply replace c by c_S in equation (9.13). In practice, as any book on solid state physics will reveal, this is a passable approximation for long wavelength (low k) phonons, although even there the velocities of transverse and longitudinal modes are very different. However, the linear dispersion must fundamentally fail at large values of k, a point related to the following.

3. There are only a limited number of phonon modes in the solid. The solid is not an elastic continuum, but consists of N atoms, so that the wavefunction of a phonon only has physical meaning (the atomic displacement) at these N atomic sites. Hence there are only $3N$ possible modes. Compare the localized oscillator model, which similarly considered $3N$ oscillators. As indicated above, the correct phonon dispersion relation will fully take care of this problem. However, this means going back to equation (4.5) and using a computer to fold in the complicated dispersion relation. An approximate fudge (the Debye model) is to maintain the linear dispersion relation, but to cut off the density of states

above a Debye cut-off frequency ν_D, defined so that:

$$3N = \int_0^{\nu_D} g(\nu)d\nu.$$

Although not in detail correct, the Debye model contains most of the important physics, and it gives the correct heat capacity of typical solids to say 10 per cent. The result for U is a modified version of equation (9.13):

$$U = V(12\pi h/c_S^3)(k_B T/h)^4 \int_0^{y(T)} y^3 dy/[\exp(y) - 1]$$

(9.14)

where $y(T) = h\nu_D/k_B T$. The heat capacity C, shown in Fig. 9.8, is obtained by differentiating equation (9.14) with respect to T.

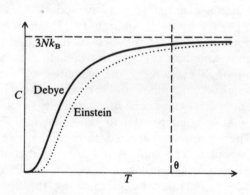

Fig. 9.8 The variation with T of the lattice heat capacity of a solid in the Debye approximation. Full curve: The Debye model (from equation (9.14)). Dotted curve: The Einstein model (Fig. 3.10), for comparison.

The introduction of the cut-off gives a scale temperature θ to the problem, defined by $k_B\theta = h\nu_D$. For most common solids θ has a value around room temperature (lower for lead, higher for diamond!). At high temperatures, $T \gg \theta$ or

$y(T) \ll 1$, the cut-off ensures that the classical limit is recovered, yielding $U = 3Nk_BT$ and $C = 3Nk_B$ (see the problems in Appendix 5). On the other hand at low temperatures, $T \ll \theta$ or $y(T) \rightarrow \infty$, we recover the result analogous to black-body radiation. The integral in equation (9.14) again becomes a constant, and we have $U \propto T^4$ and correspondingly $C \propto T^3$. This is the so-called Debye T^3 law, and is in good agreement with the experimental heat capacity of a crystalline solid at low temperatures.

Chapter 10
Entropy in other situations

As the chart in the front of the book shows, we have now completed our elementary study of the thermal equilibrium properties of ideal solids and gases. However, it would be a pity to stop here, since statistical physics has plenty more to say about other types of system also. In this chapter we shall look again at entropy, and shall discuss the statistics of a system in which the macrostate specifies T rather than U. This generalization will help us to discuss vacancies in solids in this chapter, and phase transitions in the next.

10.1 Entropy and disorder

In Chapter 1, we took as a statistical definition of entropy the relation $S = k_B \ln \Omega$ (equation (1.5)). Since many verifiable results have followed, we may by now have much confidence in the approach. In this chapter we study some further consequences of the relation.

10.1.1 Isotopic disorder

One simple form of disorder in a solid is isotopic disorder. For instance a block of copper consists of a mixture of ^{63}Cu and ^{65}Cu isotopes. Therefore, if the isotopes are randomly distributed on the lattice sites, there will be a large amount of disorder associated with all the possible arrangements of the isotopes.

Consider a solid whose N atoms have a proportion P_L of isotope L. In other words, there are $N_L = P_L N$ atoms of isotope L, and $\sum_L N_L = N$, where the sum goes over all the isotopes. The number of arrangements of isotopes on the N sites is given by the well-trodden third problem of Appendix 1. It is:

$$\Omega = N!/\prod_L N_L! \tag{10.1}$$

The calculation of S for this situation goes as follows:

$$S = k_B \ln \Omega \qquad \text{definition (1.5)}$$

$$= k_B (\ln N! - \sum_L \ln N_L!) \qquad \text{from (10.1)}$$

$$= k_B (N \ln N - \sum_L N_L \ln N_L) \qquad \begin{array}{l}\text{Stirling's} \\ \text{approx, also} \\ \sum N_L = N\end{array}$$

$$= - k_B [\sum_L N_L(\ln N_L - \ln N)] \qquad \begin{array}{l}\text{putting} \\ N = \sum N_L\end{array}$$

$$= - N k_B \sum_L P_L \ln P_L. \tag{10.2}$$

The answer (10.2) is a nice simple one. For instance if we were to have a 50–50 mixture of two isotopes, it would give an 'entropy of mixing' of $S = N k_B \ln 2$, a not unexpected result, analogous to tossing pennies (Appendix 2).

Whether this entropy is observable is another matter. In fact our block of copper does not separate out under gravity to have all the ^{65}Cu at the bottom and all the ^{63}Cu at the top, however cold it is made! Rather this disorder is frozen in, and a cold piece of copper is in a metastable state which contains this fixed amount of disorder. Therefore the entropy of isotopic disorder is usually omitted from consideration, since it has no influence on the thermal properties. Metastable states of this sort do not violate the Third Law of Thermodynamics, since no entropy *changes* occur near the absolute zero.

Actually partial isotopic separation does occur in just one case, that of liquid helium. A liquid mixture of ^3He and ^4He is entirely random above 0.8 K. However, when it is cooled below this temperature, a phase separation occurs to give a solution of almost pure ^3He floating on top of a dilute solution of about 6 per cent ^{3}He in ^{4}He. This phase separation is important to low-temperature physicists, not least because the difference in thermal properties of the ^{3}He between the two phases forms the basis of a 'dilution refrigerator', the work-horse cooling method for reaching 5 mK nowadays.

10.1.2 Localized particles

A similar calculation can be made for the entropy of an assembly of N localized particles in thermal equilibrium, the topic of Chapter 2. We have seen (equation (2.4)) that Ω, the total number of microstates, can be replaced by t^*, the number of microstates associated with the most probable distribution. Hence the entropy is given by $S = k_B \ln t^*$, with $t^* = N!/\prod n_j^*!$ (equation (2.3)). The evaluation of S exactly parallels the derivation of equation (10.2), the result being:

$$S = - Nk_B \sum_j P_j \ln P_j \qquad (10.3)$$

where $P_j = n_j/N$ (strictly n_j^*/N) is defined to be the fraction of the N particles in the state j. This important equation can be taken as an alternative statistical definition of entropy, and indeed it can be applied with greater generality than equation (1.5).

10.1.3 Gases

The same approach, of expressing S directly in terms of the distribution, can be adopted for gases, using the expressions for t^* derived in Chapter 5. Again using Stirling's approximation together with a little rearrangement, one obtains the following results:

For FD gases, from equation (5.4),

$$S = k_B \sum_i g_i [- f_i \ln f_i - (1 - f_i) \ln (1 - f_i)]. \qquad (10.4)$$

For BE gases, from equation (5.5),

$$S = k_B \sum_i g_i [- f_i \ln f_i + (1 + f_i) \ln (1 + f_i)]. \qquad (10.5)$$

For MB gases, from equation (5.6), or from the dilute $(f_i \ll 1)$ limit of equation (10.4) or equation (10.5),

$$S = k_B \sum_i g_i [-f_i \ln f_i] + Nk_B. \tag{10.6}$$

In these equations, the sums are over all groups i of states; however, another way of writing $\sum_i g_i$ is simply as a sum over all states. Therefore there is much similarity between the first (common) term of these expressions and equation (10.3) for localized particles. We may write equation (10.3) as

$$S = k_B \sum_j [-n_j \ln n_j] + Nk_B \ln N.$$

Recognizing that n_j and f_i are both defined as the number of particles per state (the filling factor), the similarity is explicit. In fact the only difference between equation (10.3) for localized particles and equation (10.6) for MB gas particles is an addition of $k_B \ln N!$ to the entropy, as we should expect from the different extensivity of the two cases (section 6.3.3).

The second terms in the FD and BE expressions are intriguing. Equation (10.4) displays that in an FD gas, one not only considers the disorder of the particles filling the states (the first term), but also of the empty states (the second term). Both terms vanish if $f_i = 0$ or 1, as is the case for each state at $T = 0$. Intuition concerning equation (10.5) is not so clearcut, except to note that some such term is a clear necessity to ensure that $S > 0$ when we now allow f_i to be > 1.

10.2 An assembly at fixed temperature

The statistical method adopted earlier in the book has been based on an assembly of particles in a macrostate of fixed number N, volume V and internal energy U. Of course for a large assembly, the specification of any macrostate in practice determines all the other thermodynamic quantities, such as temperature T, pressure P and chemical potential μ. So we have cheerfully applied our method to assemblies with a macrostate specified by (N, V, T), with little fear of anything going wrong. However, when we look back at the statistical method and its relation to entropy in particular, we shall be pointed towards a more general statistical approach, one that can be applied to new types of assembly.

Our old method is based on the properties of an *isolated system* (mechanically isolated since V is constant, thermally isolated since in addition U is constant, and of fixed particle number N). One thing we really know about an isolated system is that any internal rearrangements it makes, any spontaneous changes, will always be such as to *increase the entropy* of the system. That is the content of the second law of thermodynamics. The entropy of the equilibrium state of the isolated system is a maximum.

Now our statistical method can be viewed in exactly this way, as a theorist making changes until he finds the state of maximum entropy! We have seen that the equilibrium distribution is that with the largest number of microstates, i.e. with the maximum $t(\{n_j\})$. Our statistical mechanician fiddles with the distribution numbers until he finds the maximum t ($= t^*$). But since in the equilibrium state $S = k_B \ln t^*$, this is just the same as the maximum entropy idea of the second law. The example of section 1.6.2 is of direct relevance here. A system prepared with a non-equilibrium distribution, (i) will increase its t by adjusting the distribution, and (ii) will increase its entropy.

Having reminded ourselves of how the thermodynamic view (together with $S = k_B \ln \Omega$) is related to the statistical method for an isolated system, we now turn to consider a system at fixed temperature. Consider an assembly described by a (N, V, T) macrostate.

The condition for thermodynamic equilibrium of the (N, V, T) system is equally secure. *The free energy F must be a minimum in equilibrium*. This condition (e.g. Finn section 6.4) is again a statement of the second law. The entropy of the *universe* (i.e. of the system together with a large heat bath at temperature T) must not decrease when heat flows in or out of the system to maintain its temperature. This can be readily shown to imply that the free energy of the *system* must not increase, i.e. that it is a minimum in equilibrium.

This then suggests another approach to the statistical physics for an assembly in a way (N, V, T) macrostate. We should make (allowable) adjustments in the distribution numbers $\{n_j\}$ until F is a minimum; and this minimum in F will describe the thermodynamic state, with the corresponding $\{n_j{}^*\}$ being the equilibrium distribution. In practice, this method is straightforward for the sort of systems we have discussed previously, since we can calculate F as a function of the distribution from

$$F = U - TS = U(\{n_j\}) - k_B T \ln t(\{n_j\}). \tag{10.7}$$

An example follows in the next section. But in addition the new method enables some new problems to be attacked.

10.2.1 Distinguishable particles revisited

The new statistical method based on minimizing F (equation (10.7)) may be illustrated by rederiving the Boltzmann distribution for the situation of Chapter 2. We have N weakly interacting localized particles at a temperature T. The states of one particle are as before labelled by j.

The free energy F is given as in equation (10.7) by:

$$F = U - TS$$

$$= \sum n_j \varepsilon_j - k_B T \ln t(\{n_j\}). \tag{10.8}$$

We require to minimize F in this equation, subject now to only *one* condition, namely that $\sum n_j = N$. (There is no energy condition now since U is not restricted.) The mathematical steps are similar to those in section 2.1. The number of microstates $t(\{n_j\})$, given by equation (2.3), is substituted into (10.8). This expression for F is then differentiated, using Stirling's approximation as in equation (2.6), to give:

$$dF = \sum [\varepsilon_j + k_B T \ln n_j] dn_j. \tag{10.9}$$

Using the Lagrange method to find the minimum, we set $dF - \alpha dN = 0$, to take account of the number condition (2.8). (We have chosen to write the multiplier as $-\alpha$ simply in order to ensure below that α has its usual physical identification!). Substituting dF from equation (10.9) and removing the summation sign, the whole point of Lagrange's method, we obtain for the equilibrium distribution:

$$\varepsilon_j + k_B T \ln n_j{}^* - \alpha = 0$$

i.e. $n_j{}^* = \exp(\alpha - \varepsilon_j/k_B T)$.   (10.10)

As we should expect, this is again the Boltzmann distribution. However, there is an important difference from equation (2.12), in that now there is no β to be discussed. The $-1/k_B T$ comes in from the outset, from the macrostate. The multiplier α has the same meaning as earlier, and is determined by substituting back into the number condition $\sum n_j = N$.

10.3 Vacancies in solids

We have just seen that the free energy method gives the correct answer to an already familiar problem. That is comforting, but not very exciting. Of greater importance is that we can now tackle new problems, one of which concerns the number of vacancies which exist in equilibrium in a solid.

A vacancy occurs when an atom in the solid leaves its normal lattice position. The atom must go somewhere else,

Fig. 10.1 Two types of vacancies which can occur in solids. Case 1: surface type. Case 2: interstitial type.

as indicated in Fig. 10.1. Either the solid will expand a little, the extra atom being accommodated on a normal lattice site (case 1). Or it will sit, albeit rather uncomfortably, on an interstitial site (case 2). In the first case the vacancy will usually be formed initially at the surface and is then able to move through the solid by atomic diffusion. In the second case, both the vacancy and the interstitial defect, once formed, can diffuse through the solid. In fact the existence of vacancies is the mechanism by which atomic diffusion is able to take place, since only one atom has to move in order for a vacancy and a neighbouring atom to change places.

The question is: why do vacancies form, when clearly they require energy to do so? The answer concerns entropy, and the minimization of F. Certainly U must increase when a vacancy is formed. But at a high enough T, it is possible for this increase to be more than matched by a decrease in $(-TS)$, giving an overall lowering of F ($= U - TS$). The vacancy (and its interstitial in case 2) are free to roam, and so give considerable disorder to the solid. Note that the whole discussion here could not be started without the free energy approach, since it is T and not U which is fixed.

To be specific let us develop a simplified model of case 1 vacancies (case 2 vacancies reappear as a problem in Appendix 5). Consider a simple solid of N atoms, which contains n vacancies at temperature T. The problem is to find how n varies with T. Suppose that the formation energy of a vacancy is Φ, and that the vacancies are sufficiently dilute that they are weakly interacting. The increase in U due to the vacancies is then $n\Phi$.

The increase in entropy can be calculated in a manner similar to the isotopic disorder of section 10.1.1. The solid with n vacancies has $(N + n)$ lattice sites of which N are full and n are empty. Neglecting small surface effects, the number of possible arrangements is $(N + n)!/(N!n!)$. The increase in entropy due to the disorder of the vacancies is thus $k_B \ln [(N + n)!/N!n!]$. In practice the vibrational entropy of the solid will also increase slightly for secondary reasons, but we shall ignore this.

Following equation (10.7), the free energy increase when n vacancies are present is:

$$F(n) = U(n) - TS(n)$$

$$= n\Phi - k_B T \ln \left[(N+n)!/N!n! \right]$$
$$= n\Phi - k_B T[(N+n)\ln (N+n) - N\ln N - n\ln n].$$

Equilibrium is given by the minimum F, and there are no constraints on n. Hence the required n (strictly n^*) satisfies $dF/dn = 0$, i.e.

$$0 = dF(n)/dn$$
$$= \Phi - k_B T \ln \left[(N+n^*)/n^* \right].$$

Bearing in mind that $n^* \ll N$ (since melting has not occurred), we may replace $(N+n^*)$ by N, to give the final result for the vacancy concentration:

$$n^*/N \approx \exp (-\Phi/k_B T). \tag{10.11}$$

It is interesting that the answer is again just a simple Boltzmann factor. For most solids the value of formation energy Φ is about $1\,eV$, for example its value for copper is $1.4\,eV$. Equation (10.11) would give a vacancy concentration in copper of only about 1 in 10^{24} at room temperature (one vacancy per mole!), although in practice thermodynamic equilibrium would not be reached. Vacancy movement, i.e. diffusion, also requires an activation energy and disorder is frozen in at room temperature, another example of a metastable state. However, as the copper is heated the number of vacancies in equilibrium rises, and the time to reach equilibrium falls. By the melting point (1083°C), the number given by equation (10.11) is 1 in 10^5. For some substances, the number is even greater before melting occurs, and the increase in entropy of the solid can be observed directly as an additional heat capacity.

Chapter 11
Phase transitions

Changes of phase are of great interest, not least because of their surprise value. In this chapter we examine how statistical physics can be used to help our understanding of some phase transitions.

11.1 Types of phase transition

As mentioned earlier under our comments about the helium liquids (sections 8.3 and 9.2) phase transitions are commonly classified into 'orders'. In terms of the Gibbs free energy G ($G = U - TS + PV$ is the appropriate free energy since P and T are fixed in the phase change), a first-order transition occurs where the G surfaces for the two phases cross. The stable phase is the one with minimum G (compare the previous chapter's discussion of minimum F at fixed V and T), so that there is a jump in the first derivatives of G (i.e. S and V) at the transition. Hence 'first-order'. Furthermore supercooling and superheating effects can occur in a first-order transition, since the system can for a time be driven along the unstable (higher) branch of the G surface (see Fig. 11.1).

However, this is *not* to be the topic of this chapter. Rather we shall be discussing second-order transitions. Here the changes in G at the transition are much more gentle. As the temperature is lowered, the system as it were eases itself gradually into a new phase which grows out of the first one. There is no superheating or supercooling; it is just that the G surface has a singularity at the transition. The singularity in a

Fig. 11.1 The Gibbs free energy G around a first-order phase transition. In region A (of T and P) phase 1 is stable, whereas in region B phase 2 is stable. At the transition, jumps therefore occur in the first derivatives of G. Supercooling occurs when curve 2′ is followed (an unstable situation) below the transition; superheating corresponds to curve 1′.

true second-order transition is such that S and V are continuous, but the second derivatives of G jump. Hence there is no latent heat ($=$ change in S), but there is a jump in C (since dS/dT changes). Exact second-order transitions are rare in practice, the only good example being the transition to superconductivity of a metal in zero applied magnetic field. However, there are common examples of phase transitions which are close to second-order, namely the 'lambda transitions', like that in liquid ^{4}He (section 9.2). Other instances include transitions to ferromagnetism from paramagnetism, many transitions to ferroelectricity and some structural phase transitions from one solid phase to another.

A unifying concept for the understanding of all such transitions is that of an 'order parameter'. At high temperatures, the substance is disordered and the order parameter is zero. As one cools through the transition, the order parameter suddenly starts to grow from zero, attaining its maximum value by the time the absolute zero is reached, a state of perfect order. For the above examples, in ^{4}He (or indeed in the ideal boson gas), the order parameter is the superfluid density. For superconductivity it is the so-called energy gap. For ferromagnetism it is the spontaneous magnetization of the substance, i.e. the magnetization in zero applied field. And in the ordering of a binary alloy system (such as beta-brass, CuZn) with two types of lattice site, the order parameter characterizes which atoms are on which site.

In the sense that the onset of order in these systems is sudden, the transitions are often called 'order-disorder transitions'. The sudden onset of order implies a co-operative effect. In boson gases, the co-operation is forced by the (friendly) BE statistics. But in the other cases, the co-operation arises from interactions between the particles of the system. The importance of this chapter is that we can see how to apply statistical methods to at least one situation where the particles are *not* weakly interacting. In the next section, we shall take the transition from paramagnetism to ferromagnetism in a spin-$\frac{1}{2}$ solid as model example for these ideas.

11.2 Ferromagnetism of a spin-$\frac{1}{2}$ solid

In section 3.1, we discussed the properties of a spin-$\frac{1}{2}$ solid, an ideal paramagnetic material, in which the spins are weakly interacting. In particular (equation (3.9) and Fig. 3.8), we worked out the magnetization M of the solid as the spins line up in a magnetic field B. The result was that if $B = 0$, then $M = 0$; but if $B \gg k_B T/\mu$ then M tends to the fully aligned value $M = N\mu$, the saturation magnetization. The spontaneous magnetization $M(0)$ of the solid (defined as the magnetization in zero applied magnetic field) is zero.

For the ideal paramagnetic solid, $M(0)$ will remain zero however far the temperature is lowered (see again section 3.1.3). However, what happens in any real substance is that a phase transition occurs at some temperature T_C, driven by interactions between the spins, to an ordered state. The simplest type of order, but certainly not the only type, is ferromagnetic ordering, in which the spins all tend to align in the same direction, giving a non-zero $M(0)$. (In all this chapter we ignore domain formation–$M(0)$ refers to the magnetization in a single domain, i.e. in a not too large sample or in a not too large region of a large sample.) The degree of order in the ferromagnetic state is characterized by an order parameter m defined by:

$$m = M(0)/N\mu. \tag{11.1}$$

Our main task is to understand how m varies with temperature.

The new ingredient of this chapter is to include in the argument a treatment of the interactions between spins. How is the energy of one spin influenced by the spin state of all of the others? That simple question has a complicated answer, unless approximations are made. One extreme approximation is an 'Ising model' in which the spins are assumed only to interact with their nearest neighbours. From the present viewpoint, that is still a complicated problem even in principle, although a start can be made at it using methods to be discussed in the next chapter. The other extreme approximation is to assume that all the other spins are of equal influence, however distant they are. This is called a *mean field approximation*, and we shall see that it gives a true second-order transition.

The mean field approximation is to assume that the one-particle states of each spin are, as usual, $+\mu B$ and $-\mu B$, but the value of B is changed. Instead of being equal to B_0, the applied magnetic field, the assumption is that we may write

$$B = B_0 + \lambda M \tag{11.2}$$

where λ is a constant characteristic of the substance. This follows since M is the magnetization of *all* the spins, so the term λM averages equally over all spins in the solid. The case $\lambda = 0$ recovers the ideal paramagnet of Chapter 3. The ferromagnetic situation corresponds to a large positive value of λ, a classic case of positive feedback as we shall now see.

11.2.1 The spontaneous magnetization (method 1)

We can directly give an expression for the magnetization of the solid, using the Boltzmann distribution with the energy levels implied by equation (11.2). Following equation (3.9) the answer is:

$$M = N\mu \tanh (\mu B/k_B T)$$

$$= N\mu \tanh [\mu(B_0 + \lambda M)/k_B T]. \tag{11.3}$$

The spontaneous magnetization is obtained by setting the applied field $B_0 = 0$ in equation (11.3), giving a transcendental equation for $M(0)$. Replacing M by the dimensionless order parameter m (equation (11.1)), we obtain

$$m = \tanh (mT_C/T) \tag{11.4}$$

where

$$T_C = N\mu^2\lambda/k_B. \tag{11.5}$$

Equation (11.4) can be readily solved graphically (or numerically) as in Fig. 11.2. Plotted as the x-variable on the

Fig. 11.2 Finding the spontaneous magnetization. The solution of equation (11.4) for m is given by the intersection of the tanh curve with the straight line. Straight lines are drawn for three different temperatures.

graph is $x = mT_C/T$, so that equation (11.4) becomes $xT/T_C = \tanh x$. The solution is simply the intersection of the curve $m = \tanh x$ with the straight line $m = xT/T_C$. Since the slope of $\tanh x$ is unity close to $x = 0$, it is at once evident that:

(i) When $T > T_C$, the equation (11.4) has only one solution, namely $m = 0$. The spontaneous magnetization is zero, and the system is disordered.

(ii) $T = T_C$ is seen to be a definite transition temperature, in that below T_C other solutions are possible. T_C depends linearly on the mean field parameter λ. It is often called (for the ferromagnetic transition) the Curie temperature.

(iii) When $T < T_C$, the equation has three possible solutions. We shall see later that the $m = 0$ is now an unstable equilibrium. The solutions with $m \neq 0$ are the stable ones. Hence the solid develops below T_C a spontaneous magnetization with a definite magnitude, but with an indefinite direction.

The magnitude of m obtained by solving equation (11.4) is shown in Fig. 11.3, plotted as a function of T. The order parameter grows rapidly below T_C, reaching almost unity at $T_C/3$. One of the characteristic features of the mean field approximation is the total lack of order when $T > T_C$; the solid is effectively in a paramagnetic state in spite of the interactions between spins. However, before comparing with experiment, it is useful to rederive the result for $m(T)$ by another method.

Fig. 11.3 Variation of the order parameter m with temperature T. Note that m varies from 1 at $T = 0$ to 0 at $T = T_C$. It remains zero above T_C.

11.2.2 The spontaneous magnetization (method 2)

When in doubt, minimize the free energy! That was the burden of Chapter 10, and we can do that here, as an alternative derivation of the variation of the order parameter m with temperature. To calculate F, we find both U and S as functions of m. The internal energy contribution due to the spins is simply their potential energy in the magnetic field. With the mean field assumption (11.2), this gives

$$U = - \int_0 B \, dM$$

$$= - B_0 M - \lambda M^2 / 2. \tag{11.6}$$

In zero applied field ($B_0 = 0$) the first term of equation (11.6) vanishes, and we have as a function of m:

$$U = - (\lambda/2)(N\mu m)^2. \tag{11.7}$$

The entropy contribution from the spins can be worked our directly from equation (10.3). The fractions of the spins in the upper and lower states are given in terms of m by $P_2 = (1 - m)/2$ and $P_1 = (1 + m)/2$ respectively. [*Check*: $P_1 + P_2 = 1$, and $M = (P_1 - P_2) N\mu = N\mu m$, as required.] Hence

$$S = - N k_B (P_1 \ln P_1 + P_2 \ln P_2)$$

$$= (N k_B/2) [2 \ln 2 - (1 + m) \ln (1 + m)$$

$$- (1 - m) \ln (1 - m)]. \tag{11.8}$$

The free energy due to the spins $F = U - TS$ is now obtained by combining equations (11.8) and (11.7), together with the definition of T_C (equation (11.5)), to give:

$$F = (- N k_B/2) \{T_C m^2 + T[2 \ln 2 - (1 + m) \ln (1 + m)$$

$$- (1 - m) \ln (1 - m)]\}. \tag{11.9}$$

The stationary values of F are found by setting $dF/dm = 0$. It is a matter of elementary mathematics (try it!) to show that this leads to precisely equation (11.4), as it should. But we have learned much more from this exercise, in that we now

Fig. 11.4 Variation of F with m at various temperatures. The vertical arrows indicate the values of m for which F is a minimum at each temperature (compare Fig. 11.3).

know the full form of $F(m)$, as plotted in Fig. 11.4. We confirm that at $T > T_C$ there is just the one minimum at $m = 0$. When $T < T_C$, there are the two minima rapidly moving towards $m = +1$ and -1; and the stationary point at $m = 0$ is a maximum, an unstable position. It is also interesting to note the very shallow minimum at $T = T_C$, which indicates a very insecure equilibrium value of m; this gives an explanation of the large fluctuations often observed in the properties of a substance close to a transition point.

11.2.3 The thermal properties

The ordering of the spins is not just evident in the magnetization, but it will also give contributions to the thermal properties, for example to the entropy and to the heat capacity.

Since the variation of m with T is known (Fig. 11.3), the variation of S with T may be worked out from equation (11.8) and thence the heat capacity C from $C = T\,dS/dT$. The T-dependence of S and C in our mean field approximation are shown in Fig. 11.5. The entropy curve shows the sudden onset of order as T is reduced through T_C. Above T_C, $S = Nk_B \ln 2$ and the spins are completely disordered. Correspondingly, C vanishes above T_C, but shows a

Fig. 11.5 Entropy and heat capacity in the mean field approximation. Full curve: entropy. Dotted curve: heat capacity (vertical scale × 0.6).

considerable anomaly over the temperature region below T_C in which S is changing.

11.2.4 The paramagnetic region

Notwithstanding the zero heat capacity in the paramagnetic $(T > T_C)$ regime, we have already remarked upon the very shallow $F(m)$ curves close to the transition. Therefore, it is not surprising that the magnetic properties are affected above T_C. Although the *spontaneous* magnetization is zero, the response to an applied field is increased by the ferromagnetic interactions.

The magnetization in this region can be worked out readily as in Chapter 3. Equation (11.3) can be simplified (since B_0 and M are both small) by replacing $\tanh x$ by x to give:

$$M = N\mu\,\mu(B_0 + \lambda M)/k_B T$$

and using the definition (11.5) of T_C this rearranges to:

$$M/B_0 = N\mu^2/k_B(T - T_C). \qquad (11.10)$$

This should be compared with equation (3.10) for the ideal paramagnet. The new feature is the $-T_C$ in the denominator, which ensures that the 'paramagnetic' susceptibility does not follow Curie's law, but the so-called Curie–Weiss law. A graph of inverse susceptibility against T remains linear, but does not pass through the origin. Since $T_C > 0$ the susceptibility is everywhere increased by the interactions, and in fact diverges as the transition is approached–even a small applied field is enough to line up all the spins. This relates to the flat $F(m)$ curves, since the addition of an applied field B_0 to Fig. 11.4 (as in equation (11.6)) tilts the curves somewhat, and can move the minimum position well away from $m = 0$.

Incidentally, the same idea of tilting the $F(m)$ curves can be used in the *ferromagnetic* region to describe the influence of an applied magnetic field below T_C. One minimum becomes of lower F than the other, and the whole picture gives a good account of hysteresis curves (of M versus B_0) in a ferromagnetic material. The interested reader is referred to books on solid-state physics.

11.3   Real ferromagnetic materials

First a word of warning! We have outlined a simple theory for ferromagnetic interactions in a spin-$\frac{1}{2}$ solid.
Note: (i) In many cases the interactions in magnetic materials are antiferromagnetic, in other words neighbouring spins tend to be oppositely aligned (or to be at a non-zero angle). Ferromagnetism is not the only, and indeed not the commonest, situation. Nevertheless iron and nickel are not unknown materials, either. (ii) As in Chapter 3, extension to spins other than $\frac{1}{2}$ can readily be made, with no qualitative changes.

The mean field theory has notable successes in describing the transition from ferro- to para-magnetism. The nature of the spontaneous magnetization, the existence of a critical temperature T_C, the heat capacity anomaly and the magnetic properties are all described with reasonable accuracy. A true second-order transition (S continuous, but dS/dT discontinuous) is predicted by the theory. How does all this compare with experiment in detail?

The first comment must concern the magnitude of the parameter λ. In equation (11.2) it seems that we have assumed that λM is a real magnetic field. And in some cases it might well be so; there will always be a true magnetic coupling between the dipole moments of adjacent spins. But in the materials we think of as ferromagnets (like iron for example), the physical origin of λ comes from far stronger effects, the magnitude of λM being several hundred tesla to give T_C above room temperature. This strong coupling arises from quantum influences on the electrostatic Coulomb forces between overlapping electrons on neighbouring atoms. Since electrons are identical spin-$\frac{1}{2}$ fermions, this overlap is strongly dependent on the relative spin of the two electrons, and hence the energy of one electron is influenced by the spin of its neighbours. This gives energy splittings as suggested by equation (11.2), but the origin is not a weak magnetic one, but is due to these much larger 'exchange energies'.

Next let us consider the detailed shape of the $m(T)$ variation (Fig. 11.3). Although agreement with experiment is fair, there are two points of detail which are incorrect. At low temperatures, the mean field approach somewhat overestimates m. This is because it ignores the existence of 'spin waves', essentially long wavelength periodic variations in magnetization. These are not included in our simple theory, which is based on long-range order only, i.e. on the spins of all ranges having an equal influence. In practice spin waves do exist, and they are seen in the low temperature region both in m and also as a small additional heat capacity.

The other region of interest is close to T_C. Here the mean field theory gives too small a value of m. The transition is somewhat more catastrophic than we have predicted. The theory very close to T_C suggests $m \propto (T_C - T)^{\frac{1}{2}}$, whereas reality is closer to $m \propto (T_C - T)^{\frac{1}{3}}$. The study of such 'critical exponents' is a very searching way of understanding phase transitions.

Correspondingly, the thermal properties show deviations from Fig. 11.5, and we do not have a true second-order transition. The heat capacity shows a lambda singularity, differing from the theory in two respects. Firstly (as with m) it is more sharp just below the transition, giving a much higher value as T_C is approached. And secondly there is an additional heat capacity just above the transition (the other half of the λ-shape). These effects are thought to be due to the existence of short-range order. Above T_C, although $m = 0$ identically, i.e. there is no long-range order, we still expect neighbouring spins to interact and perhaps form transient islands of local order. (We have already noted the very large fluctuations possible here.) The paucity of the mean field approach is that, as we have seen, it treats all spins equally, whereas in reality the interaction with closer neighbours will be stronger than that from distant ones. So treatments based on, say, an Ising model will describe these details more accurately. But that would also take us beyond the scope of this chapter!

Finally (compare section 11.2.5) we can note that there is further evidence of the influence of short-range order in the magnetic properties above T_C. Until one is close to the transition, the form of equation (11.10), the Curie–Weiss law, is found to agree well with experiment. However, the parameter 'T_C' which enters it is found to be not the same as the actual ferromagnetic transition temperature, but rather a temperature a little higher (e.g. about 375 °C in nickel, compared with a T_C of 358 °C). Close to the transition it seems that M/B_0 is better described as $(T - T_C)^{-\frac{4}{3}}$, another example of mean field theory not getting the critical exponent quite right.

11.4   Order–disorder transformations in alloys

Before leaving the topic, we may note that the same type of mean field theory can be constructed for many other transitions. Here we just consider one other example, that of the phase transition which occurs in an alloy such as beta-brass CuZn.

This alloy contains equal numbers of Cu and Zn atoms. At high temperatures, the atoms lie on a body-centred cubic lattice in an entirely random arrangement. But below a transition temperature (about 460 °C), the atoms start to form an ordered arrangement, with one type of atom at the corners of each unit cell and the other type at the centre of the cell. (A body-centred cubic structure can be thought of as consisting of two interpenetrating simple cubic sub-lattices,

(a)

(b)

Fig. 11.6 Lattice sites in a crystal. The sketches show two (equivalent) types of lattice site, A and B, (a) in a square lattice in two-dimensional, and (b) in a three-dimensional body centred cubic lattice, as occurs in beta-brass.

analogous to a two-dimensional centred square lattice, illustrated in Fig. 11.6.)

The transformation can be described by the mean field approximation, with much the same success and failure as in the ferromagnetic situation. The long-range order parameter m can in this situation be defined as: $m = P_A - P_B$. Here P_A is the proportion of Cu atoms on A sites in the lattice (which is also the proportion of Zn atoms on B sites), and P_B is the proportion of Cu atoms on B sites. At high temperature, we expect $P_A = P_B = \frac{1}{2}$, so that $m = 0$. But in the fully ordered state we would have $m = +1$ or -1, depending on whether Cu or Zn occupies the A sites (another case of a 'spontaneously broken symmetry'!).

Whether the transition proceeds depends on the relative bond energy between like and unlike nearest neighbours. If it is favourable for neighbours to be unlike, we may expect a transition to occur. Writing V_{XY} as a bond energy between neighbouring X and Y atoms, we require $V = V_{CuCu} + V_{ZnZn} - 2V_{CuZn} > 0$. This parameter V plays the role of λ in the ferromagnetic situation. The mean field approximation in the present case is to assume that the number of bonds of each type is determined purely by the parameter m, assuming that the positions on the sublattices have no short-range correlations. It then follows (see the problems in Appendix 5) that the lattice internal energy can be written as $U = \text{constant} - 2NVm^2$ (compare equation (11.7)). The whole problem can then be solved as in section 11.2.

The graphs of section 11.2 may then be applied to this situation also. The ordering (i.e. $m(T)$) is easily followed by the appearance below T_C of extra lines in an X-ray powder photograph. The effects on the thermal properties are also readily measured, and there is an anomaly in C near the transition, associated with the entropy changes. As before, the anomaly in practice indicates a lambda transition, rather than the simple second-order transition of Fig. 11.5. Again, since the physical interaction is based on nearest neighbour interactions, it is not surprising that the mean field approach, with its neglect of short-range order, does not contain the full truth.

Chapter 12
Two new ideas

In this final chapter we shall explore briefly two concepts which indicate that statistical physics is not such a restrictive subject as might at first appear. The second gives clear pointers as to how we can start to deal with interacting particles. But before that, we shall consider connections between thermal equilibrium properties and transitions between states.

12.1 Statics or dynamics?

Thermal equilibrium really is all about transitions, in spite of its static (and boring?) sound. As stressed in Chapter 1, our assembly samples effectively all its possible states over the time of an experiment, otherwise the whole concept of thermal equilibrium becomes misty. The idea of a dynamic equilibrium gives all sorts of connections between equilibrium and transport properties. In this section we explore just one such connection.

12.1.1 Matter and radiation in equilibrium

This is hardly a new topic, since it was introduced by Einstein. However, it is particularly important because it brings together the properties of matter and radiation in thermal equilibrium, along with an understanding of the emission and absorption of radiation by matter.

Consider a box which contains both radiation and a number of atoms, all in thermal equilibrium at temperature T. To be specific suppose the atoms are localized particles, which have two energy states, separated by Δ [they may have other energy states also, but these are irrelevant]. Let there be N_2 atoms in the upper state, and N_1 in the lower state. One thing we have proved (Chapter 2) is that in equilibrium the ratio of the numbers of atoms in the two states is given by the Boltzmann factor:

$$N_2/N_1 = \exp\left(-\Delta/k_B T\right). \qquad \text{(2.26) and (12.1)}$$

What about the radiation? Thermal equilibrium is described in section 9.3. The photons occupy states of energy ε with an occupation function which is the modified Bose–Einstein distribution:

$$f(\varepsilon) = 1/[\exp\left(-\varepsilon/k_B T\right) - 1]. \qquad \text{(9.9) and (12.2)}$$

Let us consider the mutual equilibrium between the atoms and the photons. Clearly there can be a strong interaction between the atoms and those photons which have an energy $\varepsilon(=h\nu)=\Delta$. There can be an absorption process (atom in state $1 +$ photon of energy $\Delta \rightarrow$ atom in state 2) which conserves energy; and an emission process which is the reverse (atom in state $2 \rightarrow$ atom in state $1 +$ photon) (see Fig. 12.1).

Fig. 12.1 Matter and radiation.

Einstein's argument was to invoke the *principle of detailed balance*. This states that in equilibrium the average transition rates of absorption and emission processes must be equal (and this must be true for any transition and its inverse–

hence 'detailed' balance). Now the upward transition rate, the number of absorption processes per unit time, is plausibly given by: $R(\text{up}) = N_1 f(\Delta) g(\Delta) X$. The process needs an atom in state 1, and it needs a photon of the right energy ($g(\varepsilon)$ is the photon density of states). The factor X describes the basic coupling strength, given the correct input of atom and photon.

What can we say about $R(\text{down})$, the emission rate? It requires an atom in the upper state, so it must be proportional to N_2. And that is enough to determine it fully! Detailed balance tells us that $R(\text{down}) = R(\text{up})$, and the equilibrium distributions (equations (12.1) and (12.2)) imply that

$$N_2/N_1 [= \exp(-\Delta/k_B T)] = f(\Delta)/[1 + f(\Delta)].$$

Hence

$$R(\text{down}) = N_2 [1 + f(\Delta)] g(\Delta) X. \tag{12.3}$$

Equation (12.3) has a lot to reveal about the emission processes. The first is that the same coupling parameter X should be used for absorption and emission, an idea that should come as no surprise to anyone who has studied much quantum mechanics (the same matrix element is involved), but Einstein was inventing the subject! But of continuing interest is the $(1 + f(\Delta))$ factor in equation (12.3). The '1' term relates to what is called *spontaneous emission*, emission which will occur even if there are no other photons present. The treatment shows that it has a rate which is related both to the absorption rate and to the density of photon states into which the emission occurs. The $f(\Delta)$ term is responsible for *stimulated emission*. The emission rate is greatly increased into a photon state of the right energy, if there are already photons present in the state (those friendly bosons again!). That is the essence of laser action, in which atoms deliberately prepared to be in the upper atomic state and then de-excite by emitting photons into a cavity which supports a particular photon state. Hence the intense and coherent radiation.

Looked at from the viewpoint of statistical physics, the existence of stimulated emission is a necessity. In a strong radiation field, the stimulated term ensures that the dynamic equilibrium reached is one in which transitions up and down are frequent and $N_2 = N_1$, corresponding to infinite temperature. Disorder is rife, and the entropy is maximized. A laser needs $N_2 > N_1$, implying a negative 'temperature' i.e. a non-equilibrium prepared situation, one of lower entropy. Without the $f(\Delta)$ term in equation (12.3) one could cheat the second law; simply applying radiation would pump all the atoms up into the top state, achieving this desirable situation by equilibrium means.

12.1.2 Transitions with electrons

The principle of detailed balance may be used to establish the same sort of connection between Boltzmann statistics and Fermi–Dirac statistics. Consider as an example a metal which contains some magnetic impurities. The conduction electrons in the metal can be modelled as an ideal FD gas, which we know in thermal equilibrium will have the distribution of equation (8.2). The magnetic impurities can again be considered as a number of atoms with two energy states separated by Δ. As before, their equilibrium distribution is to be given by equation (12.1).

The transitions in question are inelastic scattering processes of an electron from the impurity atom. In an 'up' transition (of the atom, as previously) an atom in the lower state collides with an electron of energy $(\varepsilon + \Delta)$ leaving the atom in the upper state and the electron with energy ε. The reverse 'down' transition sees the atom go from state 2 to state 1, whilst the electron energy increases from ε to $(\varepsilon + \Delta)$.

Detailed balance should apply to every transition, whatever electron energy ε is involved. Since the electrons are fermions obeying the exclusion principle, the requirements for the up transition are, (i) an atom in state 1, (ii) a filled electron state of energy $(\varepsilon + \Delta)$, and (iii) an empty electron state of energy ε. Hence, in the spirit of the previous section, we would expect the transition rates to be:

$$R(\text{up}) = N_1 f(\varepsilon + \Delta)[1 - f(\varepsilon)]g(\varepsilon + \Delta)g(\varepsilon)X$$

and $$R(\text{down}) = N_2 f(\varepsilon)[1 - f(\varepsilon + \Delta)]g(\varepsilon + \Delta)g(\varepsilon)X$$

$$(12.4)$$

where $f(\varepsilon)$ is the distribution and $g(\varepsilon)$ the density of states for electrons of energy ε. The factor X is again the appropriate coupling strength for the transition under examination. Now using detailed balance $R(\text{up}) = R(\text{down})$, and assuming $N_2/N_1 = \exp(-\Delta/k_B T)$, it follows from equations (12.4) that the distribution function for the electrons must be of the form:

$$[1 - f(\varepsilon)]/f(\varepsilon) = B \exp(\varepsilon/k_B T)$$

with B a constant (independent of ε). This rearranges to give

$$f(\varepsilon) = 1/[B \exp(\varepsilon/k_B T) + 1]$$

which is precisely the FD distribution (equation (8.2)), as indeed it should be. The argument of this section can be seen either as an alternative derivation of the FD distribution, or as a confirmation of the principle of detailed balance. We may further note that similar arguments can be made (with equally satisfactory results) for transitions of the atoms involving instead of electrons either massive bosons or other Boltzmann particles.

12.2 Ensembles – a larger view

Statistical physics has many possible entry points. In this book, we have concentrated on one of the least abstract routes, that which concentrates on a piece of matter modelled by the (N, U, V) macrostate. The assembly under consideration consists of N weakly interacting particles, and the total energy U is fixed. Both of these limitations are essential for the method of Chapter 1 onwards to make sense.

But here is the new idea. Let us raise the scale of our thoughts, and apply the identical methods to a larger universe. Previously, we had;

an assembly of N identical particles with a fixed total energy U.

Now we shall consider:

as 'ensemble' of N_A identical assemblies with a fixed total energy $N_A U$.

Why? Who wants to consider 10^{23} or so blocks of copper, when we are only really interested in one of them? The answer, of course, concerns averaging. We are interested in the average properties of one assembly, and this ensemble is one way of letting nature do the averaging for us! We can think of the ensemble as consisting of one assembly (whose thermodynamic properties we wish to know) in a heat reservoir provided by all the others, so that this is a way of modelling an assembly at fixed *temperature*, rather than the old method of fixed energy.

Furthermore, our statistical method applies immediately and precisely to this ensemble. The assemblies are separate macroscopic entities, so they are distinguishable 'particles' without a doubt. They can be placed in as weak contact as necessary, so the 'weakly interacting' limitation is unimportant. And we can avoid any doubts about numerical approximations by making N_A effectively infinite – after all, the ensemble is a figment of the imagination, not a blueprint for a machinist. Hence, the Boltzmann distribution (Chapter 2) applies.

For the assembly of particles, we derived the Boltzmann distribution:

$$n_j = (N/Z) \exp\left(-\varepsilon_j/k_B T\right) \qquad (2.23)$$

with the partition function being

$$Z = \sum_j \exp\left(-\varepsilon_j/k_B T\right) \qquad (2.24)$$

the label j going over all one-particle states.

The parallel result for the ensemble involves the energy states of one assembly. Since an assembly is itself a large and complex entity, it has very many states of a particular energy. In fact, these are the *microstates* of Chapter 1; an assembly of energy E_j has $\Omega(E_j, V, N)$ such states. Since the allowed values of E are very close indeed, we usually adopt the density of states approximation and define $G(E)\delta E$ as the number of one-assembly states (= microstates) with energy between E and $E + \delta E$. The assembly partition function Z_A is defined as the sum over all one-assembly states of the Boltzmann factors, i.e.

$$Z_A = \sum \Omega(E_j, V, N) \exp(-E_j/k_B T) \qquad (12.5a)$$

or $\quad Z_A = \int_0^\infty G(E) \exp(-E/k_B T)\, dE. \qquad (12.5b)$

The distribution is specified by the number $N(E)\delta E$ of the N_A assemblies in the usual energy range, or rather more usefully by the proportion $P(E)\delta E = N(E)\delta E/N_A$. The Boltzmann result then becomes:

$$P(E) = N(E)/N_A = G(E) \exp(-E/k_B T)/Z_A. \qquad (12.6)$$

As before we may use equations (12.5) and (12.6) to calculate the thermodynamic functions for the ensemble – and hence for the average assembly. We write the total free energy as $N_A F$ and the total entropy as $N_A S$ (compare the definition U above). Thus the symbols U, S and F refer to the required average values per assembly. Following the 'royal route' of Chapter 2, we obtain for the average assembly:

$$F = -k_B T \ln Z_A. \qquad (12.7) \text{ compare } (2.28)$$

Hence all the thermal properties of the assembly may be calculated from the microstates.

Several comments follow concerning the new viewpoint as expressed in the three equations (12.5), (12.6) and (12.7).

1. *Temperature.* The value of T which appears in the equations is determined from the properties of the whole ensemble (just as β in Chapter 2 was a property of the whole assembly). Therefore, as remarked above, when we concentrate on the behaviour of just one assembly we are discussing

its properties when in contact with a large (conceptually infinite) heat reservoir at this temperature T.

2. *Internal energy.* Although T is fixed by the ensemble, the internal energy of any one assembly is not. The energy of an assembly can have any value E, with a probability given by equation (12.6). The one thing we can be sure about is that the *average* value of E is U, for that was one of the starting points. However, equation (12.6) contains the full statistical information about E, and that we shall now examine in greater detail.

3. *The distribution function $P(E)$.* For assemblies of any reasonable size, it turns out that $P(E)$ is a very strongly peaked function indeed around its maximum value (which thus effectively equals the mean value U). This comes about because the assembly 'density of microstates' function $G(E)$ is a rapidly rising function of E, whereas the exponential factor in equation (12.6) is a rapidly falling function. Consider (without working the problem out in detail) a specific case, where the answer is already well known from Chapter 6. This is where each assembly consists of N dilute gas particles, to which MB statistics apply. Suppose that $G(E) \propto E^n$. Then (equation (12.6)) $P(E) \propto E^n \exp(-E/k_B T)$. The maximum is given by $dP/dE = 0$, i.e. (check it!) when $E = nk_B T$. In our example we know that $U = (\frac{3}{2})Nk_B T$, so the index n must equal to $3N/2$. This is a fantastically high power for the rising factor. Correspondingly the falling exponential factor has an exponent $-3N/2$, quite enough to frighten any normal calculator.

4. *Fluctuations.* Continuing the previous point, $P(E)$ also enables us to work out the probable fluctuations of E around the mean value U. The sharpness of the maximum is readily characterized from the second derivative d^2P/dE^2 at the maximum. A Taylor expansion of $P(E)$ about the maximum shows that a useful measure of the width ΔE of the curve is given by $d^2P/dE^2 = P(U)/(\Delta E)^2$. For the above example, this gives $\Delta E = n^{\frac{1}{2}}k_B T$, or more usefully the fractional width $\Delta E/U = 1/\sqrt{n} \approx 1/\sqrt{N}$. The relative fluctuations in E are large for a small assembly at a fixed temperature, but reduce

as about $1/\sqrt{N}$ for a large assembly at a given T.

5. *The same answers for the same problems.* Naturally since no new assumptions have been made, the problems we have already tackled will still have the same solutions attacked by the new method. For instance let us consider an assembly of N distinguishable particles as in Chapter 2. We can calculate Z_A by one of two methods.

(i) We can use the ideas of the factorization of a partition function elaborated in our discussion of diatomic gases (section 7.1). Since the particles are weakly interacting, the microstate simply specifies the state of each individual particle in turn, and the various one-particle energies (all N of them) simply add to give E, the assembly energy. Therefore the assembly partition function (equation (12.5a)) is given simply by

$$Z_A = Z^N$$

each particle contributing a factor Z (equation (2.24)). We can immediately check that this is correct, since $F = -k_B T \ln Z_A$ (equation (12.7)) $= -Nk_B T \ln Z$ (identical to equation (2.28)).

(ii) We may also calculate Z_A using equation (12.5a) together with the multinomial theorem (Appendix 1). Because the coefficients $t(\{n_j\})$ are identical (for an assembly of distinguishable particles) to the multinomial coefficients, it is not too hard to prove that the sum in equation (12.5a) can be performed explicitly; and that the result again is Z^N.

Method (ii) is worth examining in addition to method (i), since when we come to gases method (i) is not available. The gas particles are competing for the same states, so Z_A cannot factorize into a factor from each particle. However, method (ii) gives us the answer for a dilute (MB) gas. (The calculation of Z_A for FD and BE gases requires yet further work, which we shall not pursue here.) The values of $t(\{n_j\})$ for the MB gas simply differ by that factor $N!$ from those for the distinguishable Boltzmann particles. Therefore the summation goes through unscathed, except for this constant factor throughout, to give

$$Z_A = Z^N/N!$$

for the assembly partition function. This expression, when put into equation (12.7), gives $F = -Nk_BT \ln Z + k_BT \ln N!$, identical to the result of Chapter 6 (equation (6.16)).

6. *A way into new problems.* The importance of the new method is that a wider range of assemblies can now be studied, at any rate in principle. The three equations (12.5), (12.6) and (12.7) outline a programme which should work for an ensemble of any assemblies. The equations make no restrictions on 'what is inside each box', the only requirement being that we have in mind a large number of identical boxes. So the assembly could contain interacting particles, and still the method would be the same. Naturally it becomes mathematically difficult, but at least the physics is clear. The computational problem is immense, as soon as the energy E depends on interactions between the 10^{23} particles. Nobody can yet fully work out the properties of a liquid from first principles. However, some progress can be made. For example, the small deviations from the ideal gas laws for real gases (which are only slightly non-ideal) can be related to the interaction potential between two gas particles, using expansion methods effectively in powers of the interaction. Another tractable problem is that of the Ising model, mentioned as a (more physical?) alternative to the mean field approximation of Chapter 11. Here we have a solid in which only nearest neighbours interact, so that the expression for E is not too desperate. In fact it is exactly soluble in two dimensions, and satisfactory numerical results can be obtained in three dimensions.

7. *Nomenclature.* You know the methods, so why not learn their names? (At least it helps to impress your friends!) The ensemble of this chapter, with a probability function for E given by equation (12.6), is called the *canonical ensemble*. The earlier method of the book can also be thought of as involving an ensemble (see section 1.3); but now each

assembly of the ensemble had the same energy U. In the language of equation (12.6), $P(E)$ for the ensemble is a delta-function at energy U. This is called the *micro-canonical ensemble*.

8. *New horizons*. Finally, we can point out that the degree of abstraction need not end here. In the canonical ensemble, the restriction that U is fixed is removed, in comparison to the micro-canonical ensemble. But the assemblies are still constrained to have a given number N of particles. For some purposes this is quite unphysical. For example consider the properties of a litre of air in the middle of the room. The properties of this 'open assembly' are thermodynamically well defined and calculable. We can describe its properties in statistical physics with a *grand canonical ensemble* which consists of an array of these open assemblies. Now there is not only energy exchange between assemblies, but there is also particle exchange. What happens now is that the whole ensemble defines a chemical potential μ, determined by the total number of particles in the ensemble, just as T in the canonical ensemble was determined by the total energy $(N_A U)$ of the ensemble. In the grand canonical ensemble, an assembly may have any number of particles, but, as one might anticipate, there is again a very sharp probability function $P(E, N)$ which ensures that E and N are in practice well defined. As with the canonical ensemble, the grand canonical ensemble solves all our old problems equally well. But in addition it opens new techniques, essential, for example, for discussing chemical reactions and equilibrium and for a study of solutions.

Appendix 1
Some elementary counting problems

Suppose you have N distinguishable objects.

1. *In how many different ordered sequences can they be arranged?*

The answer is $N!$

The explanation is not hard, but in this case as always the reader is encouraged to test the result with a few simple examples (e.g. try arranging three objects, A, B and C, and identify the $3! = 6$ arrangements). In general you should convince yourself that in first position in the sequence there are N choices of object; in second place (having made the first-place choice) there are $N - 1$; and so on, until for the Nth place there is just one object left to choose. Hence the required result is $N \times (N - 1) \times (N - 2) \ldots 1$, i.e. $N!$.

2. *In how many ways can the N objects be split up into two piles, ordering within the piles being unimportant? The first pile is to contain n objects and the second m.*

The answer is obviously zero, unless $n + m = N$. If the numbers do add up, then the answer is $N!/(n! \times m!)$.

The zero answer may seem trivial, but it is analogous to the requirements of getting the total number of particles right in a statistical distribution. There are several ways of seeing the correct answer, of which one is as follows. Call the required number t. We can recognize that the $N!$ arrangements (problem 1) can be partitioned so that the first n placed objects are put into the first pile, and the remaining m

placed objects into the second pile. However, these $N!$ arrangements will not all give distinct answers to the present question, since the order within each pile is unimportant. Hence, we can see that

$$N! = t \times n! \times m! \tag{A1.1}$$

where the $n!$ and $m!$ factors allow for this disordering (again using the result of problem 1). Again convince yourself with a small-number example.

Before leaving the problem, it is important to recognize that it is identical to the binomial theorem question: what is the coefficient of $x^n y^m$ in the expansion of $(x + y)^N$? And the answer is the same: zero unless $n + m = N$, but if $n + m = N$ then the required number is $N!/(n! \times m!)$.

3. *In how many ways can the N objects be arranged if they are now split up into r piles, with n_j objects in pile number j (j = 0, 1, 2, . . . r)?*

The answer is zero unless $N = \Sigma n_j$. If the n_js do sum to N then the required number of ways is $N!/(n_0!n_1!...n_r!)$.

This result follows as a straightforward extension of the proof of problem 2, equation (A1.1) becoming: $N! = t \times \prod n_j$. This important result is the one used extensively in Chapter 2.

Again one may note that this problem may be thought of (and solved) as the question of the multinomial theorem: what is the coefficient of $y_0^{n_0} y_1^{n_1} y_2^{n_2} \ldots$ in the expansion of $(y_0 + y_1 + y_2 + \ldots)^N$? And the answer is identical.

Appendix 2
Some problems with large numbers

1. Stirling's Approximation

Stirling's approximation gives a very useful method for dealing with factorials of large numbers. The form in which it should be known and used in statistical physics is:

$$\ln X! = X \ln X - X \qquad (A2.1)$$

for any large integer X. And another useful result may be obtained by differentiating (A2.1) to give:

$$d(\ln X!)/dy = (dX/dy)\{\ln X + 1 - 1\}$$

$$= (dX/dy)\ln X \qquad (A2.2)$$

where one assumes that X may be considered a continuous variable.

Equation (A2.1) is not difficult for the interested party to prove. Consider the definite integral $I = \int_1^X \ln z \, dz$. Integration by parts expresses this as $[z \ln z - z]_1^X$, which when evaluated between the limits gives:

$$I = X \ln X - X + 1.$$

However, a quick inspection of a graph of this integral (Fig. A2.1) shows that the integral (i.e. the area under the curve) lies almost midway between the areas of the two staircases on the diagram. And the upper staircase has an area of $(\ln 1 + \ln 2 + \ldots + \ln X) = \ln X!$.

Therefore we see that $I = \ln X!$ – an error term of approximately $(\frac{1}{2})\ln X$.

Fig. A2.1 Stirling's approximation.

The lower one's area is

$$[\ln 1 + \ln 2 + \ldots + \ln (X-1)] = \ln (X-1)!$$
$$= \ln X! - \ln X.$$

Hence: $\ln X! = X \ln X - X[+ (\tfrac{1}{2}) \ln X + \text{term of order unity}]$.
This is Stirling's approximation. It really is remarkably accurate for the sort of numbers we use in statistical physics; even for a very modest $X = 1000$, the error in using equation (A2.1) is less than 0.1 per cent, and the fractional error goes roughly as $1/X$.

2. A problem with pennies

An unbiased penny is tossed N times. (i) How many possible arrangements of heads (H) and tails (T) are there? (ii) What is the most probable number of H and T after the N tosses? (iii) What is its probability? In particular what is this probability when N is large?

This problem bears much similarity to the statistical physics at high temperatures of a spin-$\tfrac{1}{2}$ solid (section 3.1), and we shall apply the usual nomenclature in discussing it. The answer to the first problem is simply 2^N ($= \Omega$, say, by analogy), since each toss has two possibilities. The answer to problem (ii) is also readily solved since the coin is unbiased. This means that each of the 2^N arrangements (or microstates) has equal probability; hence the most probable distribution of H and T is that which includes the most microstates. And that is the distribution with equal numbers of heads and tails (we assume N to be even for convenience!). This is readily proved from problem 2 of Appendix 1. A distribution of n H and m $(= N - n)$ T can occur in $t = N!/(n!m!)$ ways, and this is maximized when $n = m = N/2$.

Problem (iii) is then also solved. The required probability P is given by t^*/Ω, i.e. $P = N!/\{(N/2)!^2 2^N\}$. However, the interest and the relevance to statistical physics come when we evaluate P when N is large. Here is the calculation:

$$
\begin{aligned}
\ln P &= \ln N! - 2\ln (N/2)! - N\ln 2 && \text{from above} \\
&= N\ln N - N - 2(N/2)\ln (N/2) && \text{from (A2.1)} \\
&\quad + 2(N/2) - N\ln 2 \\
&= 0. && \text{since every-} \\
& && \text{thing cancels!}
\end{aligned}
$$

Hence $\ln P = 0$, or $P = 1$, within the accuracy of Stirling's approximation. Another way of stating this result is as: $t^* = \Omega$, a result we have used in Chapter 2 and elsewhere. Since we have noted the success of (A2.1) we can have confidence in our statistical method.

However, before leaving this example, a word of warning. It is not in fact true that the probability of getting *exactly* $N/2$ H and $N/2$ T increases towards 1 as N increases! Rather $\ln P$ gets smaller as $\ln N$ (the error in (A2.1)), as may be verified by anyone with a microcomputer and a sense of adventure. But the sharpness of the probability at the maximum does increase as N gets larger, defined say by the probability of getting a distribution within 0.1 per cent of the most probable. In other words it is the probability of getting *nearly* the most probable which becomes overwhelmingly large, on any reasonable definition of 'nearly'. Fortunately, this is precisely the sort of situation in which we are interested in statistical physics.

Appendix 3
Some useful integrals

1. Maxwell–Boltzmann integrals

To calculate the properties of a MB gas, as in Chapter 6, we need to evaluate the definite integrals of the form:

$$I_n = \int_0^\infty y^n \, exp \, (-by^2) \, dy \qquad (A3.1)$$

where n is any positive integer. This can be done in three stages.

(i) Equation (A3.1) may be integrated by parts to give

$$I_n = [y^{n-1} \exp (-by^2)/2b]_0^\infty + [(n-1)/2b]I_{n-2}.$$

For $n \geq 2$, the first term is zero since it vanishes at both limits, giving a simple recurrence relation between I_n and I_{n-2}:

$$I_n = [(n-1)/2b]I_{n-2}. \qquad (A3.2)$$

For some purposes, for example the calculation of the rms speed of gas molecules, the recurrence relation contains enough information by itself. But equation (A3.2) is useful in every case, since its application reduces any integral I_n to a known multiple of either I_1 or I_0.

(ii) The integral I_1 is obtained by simple integration, the result being

$$I_1 = 1/2b. \qquad (A3.3)$$

(iii) The integral I_0 takes a little longer to evaluate. A quick method is to consider a two-dimensional problem, to integrate $\exp(-br^2)$ over the whole $x-y$ plane, r being the distance from the origin. We know from the definition (A3.1) that

$$2I_0 = \int_{-\infty}^{\infty} \exp(-bx^2)\,dx = \int_{-\infty}^{\infty} \exp(-by^2)\,dy.$$

Hence

$$4I_0^2 = \int_{-\infty}^{\infty}\int_{-\infty}^{\infty} \exp[-b(x^2+y^2)]\,dx\,dy$$

$$= \int_0^{\infty} \exp(-br^2)2\pi r\,dr$$

$$= 2\pi I_1$$

$$= \pi/b$$

Thus $I_0 = (\tfrac{1}{2})\surd(\pi/b)$. \hfill (A3.4)

The three equations (A3.2), (A3.3) and (A3.4) between them enable one to evaluate any of the required integrals.

2. Fermi–Dirac integrals

In Chapter 8, we gave several results for the properties of an ideal FD gas in the limit $T \ll T_F$. The calculations require the (approximate) evaluation of integrals of the form:

$$I = \int_0^{\infty} [dF(\varepsilon/d\varepsilon]f(\varepsilon)\,d\varepsilon \hfill (A3.5)$$

The function $F(\varepsilon)$ is chosen to suit the property required, and $f(\varepsilon)$ is the FD distribution, equation (8.2). Integration by parts of equation (A3.5) gives

$$I = -F(0) - \int_0^{\infty} F(\varepsilon)[df(\varepsilon)/d\varepsilon]\,d\varepsilon \hfill (A3.6)$$

where we have used $f(0) = 1$ and $f(\infty) = 0$. Usually one can choose the ('user-defined') function so that $F(0) = 0$, so we shall ignore the first term of equation (A3.6). The function $(-df/d\varepsilon)$ is an interesting one in the limit $k_B T \ll \mu$. It is zero except within about k_BT of the Fermi energy, and in fact behaves like a 'delta-function' with a non-zero width. (At $T = 0$ it becomes identical to the delta function.) Therefore equation (A3.6) is evaluated by expanding the function $F(\varepsilon)$ as a Taylor series about μ, since only its properties close to $\varepsilon = \mu$ are relevant. The result is

$$I = F(\mu) + (\pi^2/6)(k_BT)^2 F''(\mu) + \dots. \tag{A3.7}$$

Note that, (i) the first term, the value of F at the Fermi level, is the only one to survive at $T = 0$; that is the delta-function property, (ii) there is no first derivative term since $(-\,df/d\varepsilon)$ is symmetrical about the Fermi level; and hence no term linear in T, and (iii) the first correction to the zero temperature value is proportional to T^2. If $F(\varepsilon)$ is a reasonable power law of ε, then it will have a magnitude of order $(k_BT/\mu)^2$ times the first term. The factor $(\pi^2/6)$ which enters comes from the definite integral

$$\int_0^\infty y^2 \exp(y)\,dy/[1 + \exp(y)]^2 = \pi^2/6$$

(which is one of those integrals a physicist may look up, rather than prove?). The expression for $\mu(T)$ given at the end of section 8.1.2 is obtained from equation (A3.7) using $F(\varepsilon) = \int_0 g(\varepsilon)\,d\varepsilon$. And equation (8.9) for $U(T)$ is obtained with $F(\varepsilon) = \int_0 \varepsilon g(\varepsilon)\,d\varepsilon$.

Appendix 4
Some useful constants

Boltzmann's constant	$k_B = 1.38 \times 10^{-23}\,\mathrm{J\,K^{-1}}$
Avogadro's number	$N_A = 6.02 \times 10^{23}\,\mathrm{mol^{-1}}$
Gas constant	$R = 8.31\,\mathrm{J\,mol^{-1}\,K^{-1}}$
Planck's constant	$h = 6.63 \times 10^{-34}\,\mathrm{J\,s}$
	$\hbar = h/2\pi = 1.05 \times 10^{-34}\,\mathrm{J\,s}$
Electronic charge	$e = 1.60 \times 10^{-19}\,\mathrm{C}$
Speed of light	$c = 3.00 \times 10^{8}\,\mathrm{m\,s^{-1}}$
Mass of electron	$m = 9.11 \times 10^{-31}\,\mathrm{kg}$
Mass of proton	$M_P = 1.67 \times 10^{-27}\,\mathrm{kg}$
Bohr magneton $(= e\hbar/2m)$	$\mu_B = 9.27 \times 10^{-24}\,\mathrm{J\,T^{-1}}$
Nuclear magneton $(= e\hbar/2M_P)$	$\mu_N = 5.05 \times 10^{-27}\,\mathrm{J\,T^{-1}}$
Atmospheric pressure	$= 1.01 \times 10^{5}\,\mathrm{Pa}$ (i.e. $\mathrm{N\,m^{-2}}$)
Molar volume of ideal gas at STP	$= 22.4 \times 10^{-3}\,\mathrm{m^3}$
Permeability of free space	$\mu_0 = 4\pi \times 10^{-7}\,\mathrm{H\,m^{-1}}.$

Appendix 5
Questions

Chapter 1

1 Consider a model thermodynamic assembly in which the allowed (non-degenerate) one-particle states have energies 0, ε, 2ε, 3ε, 4ε,.... The assembly has four distinguishable (localized) particles and a total energy of 6ε. Identify the nine possible distributions, evaluate Ω and work out the *average* distribution of the four particles in the energy states. (See also Chapter 5, question 1.)

Chapter 2

1 Verify equation (2.28), (a) by working through the outline derivation given in the text, and (b) by using it to derive an expression for $S[=-(\partial F/\partial T)_{V,N}]$ which is the same as that obtained by method 1 of section 2.5.

Chapter 3

1 Below what temperature will there be deviations of greater than 5 per cent from Curie's law (equation (3.10)), even in an ideal spin-$\frac{1}{2}$ solid?

2 The magnetization of Pt nuclei (spin $\frac{1}{2}$) is commonly used as a thermometric quantity at very low temperatures. The measuring field is $10\,\text{mT}$, and the value of μ for Pt is $0.60\,\mu_N$. Estimate the useful range for the thermometer, assuming, (a) that a magnetization of less than 10^{-4} of the maximum cannot be reliably measured, and (b) that deviations from Curie's law of greater than 5 per cent (see Question 1) are unacceptable. In practice NMR techniques are used to single out the energy splitting; what is the NMR frequency in this case?

3 Negative temperatures? Show that for the spin-$\frac{1}{2}$ solid with thermal energy $U(\text{th})$, the temperature is given by $1/T = (k_B/\varepsilon) \ln \{[N\varepsilon - U(\text{th})]/U(\text{th})\}$. Hence show that negative temperatures would be reached if $U(\text{th}) > N\varepsilon/2$.

(a) A mad scientist, bowled over with the logic of equation (3.7), suggests that it should be possible to achieve negative temperatures in the spin system by an adiabatic reversal of the applied field (i.e. demagnetization and remagnetization with B reversed). Explain why this method will not work. (*Hints*: Plot temperature versus time for the process; and Fig. 3.7 should help also.)

(b) A negative temperature in a spin system can nevertheless be reached; indeed it is a prerequisite for a laser or maser. Look up and write a brief account of the methods used.

(c) Explain why negative temperatures cannot be contemplated in the assembly of harmonic oscillators.

4 The energy levels of a localized particle are 0, ε, 2ε. The middle level is doubly degenerate (i.e. two quantum states have this same energy) and the other levels are singly degenerate. Write down and simplify the partition function. Hence compare the thermal properties (U, C, S) an assembly of these particles with the properties of the spin-$\frac{1}{2}$ solid.

5 Explain why iron is not used as the coolant for adiabatic demagnetization.

Chapter 4

1 Consider waves trapped in, (a) a one-dimensional, and (b) a two-dimensional box. In each case, derive $g(k)\delta k$ and compare your results with equation (4.4). Find the energy dependence of the density of states in ε for a gas of particles of mass M, comparing with equation (4.9).

Chapter 5

1 Repeat Question 1 of Chapter 1 for a model assembly of four particles with the same energy states and with $U = 6\varepsilon$ as before, for the cases when the particles are, (a) gaseous bosons, and (b) gaseous fermions. Compare the results for the three cases.

2 (Not an easy problem.) As a game–which has no physical basis–work out the statistics of a gas obeying 'intermediate statistics'. The one-particle states of the gas may be occupied by 0, 1, 2, ... $p-1$, p particles, so that the two physical cases are $p = 1$ (FD) and p infinite (BE). Obtain expressions for $t\{(n_i)\}$ and for the thermal distribution, valid for any specified value of p. Check that the two limits give the correct results. (*Hint*: If you get stuck, see if your library has *Molecular Physics*, vol. 5 p. 525 (1962) in which all is revealed!)

Chapter 6

1 Check the derivation of equation (6.8) from (6.7), including the value of the constant C.

2 Using the integrals of Appendix 3, verify the stated expressions for the mean and the rms speeds in section 6.2.

3 What is the distribution function in v_x for a MB gas? This is defined such that $n(v_x)\mathrm{d}v_x$ is the number of particles with x-component of velocity between v_x and $v_x + \mathrm{d}v_x$.

4 In an experiment to study the MB distribution, gas molecules are observed after they have escaped through a small hole in the oven. Show that the rms speed of the escaped molecules equals $2v_T$ (i.e. higher than the rms speed inside the oven). (*Hint*: Do question 3 first?).

5 Find the constant in equation (6.10).

Chapter 7

1 Calculate the percentage contribution of vibration to the heat capacity of O_2 gas at room temperature (293 K). The characteristic (Einstein) temperature for vibration in O_2 is 2200 K.

2 Work out the characteristic temperatures of rotation (equation (7.7)) for, (a) O_2, (b) H_2, (c) D_2, (d) HD. The masses of H, D and O are respectively 1, 2 and 16 times

M_P. The internuclear distance in O_2 is 1.20×10^{-10} m, and in the hydrogen gases is 0.75×10^{-10} m.

3 Consider the properties of D_2. (a) Show that the A spin states (i.e. para-deuterium) are associated with odd-l rotational states, and the S spin states (ortho-deuterium) with even-l rotational states. (b) What is the ortho:para ratio in deuterium at room temperature? (c) What is the equilibrium composition at low temperatures?

4 Suppose the partition function Z of a MB gas depends on V and T as $Z \propto V^x T^y$. Find P and C_V.

Chapter 8

1 Check the derivation of equation (8.5). Hence work out the Fermi energy and Fermi temperature of the conduction electrons in metallic copper. You may assume that the conduction electrons behave as an ideal gas of free electrons, one electron per atom. The molar volume of copper is 7 cm^3. Show from a calculation of the Fermi velocity of the electrons (defined by $\hbar k_F = m v_F$) that relativistic corrections are not important.

2 Calculate the Fermi temperature for liquid ^{3}He, assuming the ideal gas model. The molar volume of liquid ^{3}He is 35 cm^3.

3 Verify equation (8.8), that the average energy per particle in an ideal FD gas is $(\frac{3}{5})\mu$. Prove in addition that the average speed of the gas particles (at $T = 0$) is $(\frac{3}{4})v_F$, where the Fermi velocity v_F is defined by $m v_F = \hbar k_F$.

4 A semiconductor can often be modelled as an ideal FD gas, but with an 'effective mass' of the carriers differing from the free electron mass m. A particular sample of InSb has a carrier density of 10^{22} m^{-3}, with effective mass $0.014\,m$. You may assume that the carrier density does not vary significantly with temperature (more or less valid for this material). (a) Find $\mu(0)$ and T_F. (b) Show that at room temperature (say 300 K) MB statistics may just be safely used. (c) Estimate μ at 300 K. (*Hint*: it will be negative–why? Note that the power series method of Appendix 3 cannot be applied accurately here.) How does μ vary with T above 300 K?

Chapter 9

1 Work through the steps leading to equations (9.3) and (9.4).

2 Estimate the condensation temperature T_B for an ideal BE gas of the same density of ^{4}He atoms as occurs in liquid ^{4}He (molar volume $27 \, cm^3$).

3 The Stefan–Boltzmann law states that the energy flux radiated from a black body at temperature T is $\sigma T^4 \, Jm^{-2}s^{-1}$. Derive this law from first principles, assuming that the radiation may be described as a photon gas. (a) Explain the origin of the T^4 factor. (b) Compare your theoretical value of σ with the experimental value, $\sigma = 5.67 \times 10^{-8} \, Wm^{-2}K^{-4}$.

4 A vacuum insulated flask has the shape of a sphere (with a narrow neck!) of volume $5 \times 10^{-3} m^3$. The flask is filled with liquid nitrogen (boiling point $77 \, K$, latent heat $1.70 \times 10^8 \, Jm^{-3}$). (a) Estimate the hold time of the flask (important practically if the flask is used as a 'cold trap'), assuming that the outer surface of the flask is at $300 \, K$ and that both surfaces behave as perfect black bodies. (b) How in practice is such a (thermos) flask made more efficient? Explain.

5 Wien's law for black-body radiation (used for thermometry by colour) states that $\lambda_{max} T = $ constant, where λ_{max} refers to the maximum in $u(\lambda)$, the energy density per unit wavelength. The experimental value of Wien's constant is about $0.0029 \, Km$. Calculate the theoretical value of the constant as follows:

(a) Re-express Planck's law (equation (9.12)) in terms of wavelength λ instead of frequency ν. Explain why the peaks in $u(\nu)$ and in $u(\lambda)$ do not occur at the same photon states.

(b) Using the usual type of dimensionless variable $y = ch/\lambda k_B T$ obtain an equation for y_{max}, the y-value corresponding to λ_{max}.

(c) Solve the equation numerically or graphically. (*Hint*: the solution occurs at y just less than 5.) Hence compute Wien's constant.

(d) Show that the maximum in equation (9.12) occurs at a y-value just less than 3, as mentioned in the text.

6 Starting from equation (9.14) for the thermal energy of a solid: (a) Show that at high temperatures, the classical result $C_V = 3Nk_B$ is recovered. (*Hint*: only small values of y are involved, so expand the exponential.) (b) Show that the Debye T^3 follows at low temperatures. (c) At even lower temperatures, equation (9.14) will become invalid because it is based on the density of states approximation. Estimate the temperature below which equation (9.14) will severely overestimate U (and hence C_V) for a sample of size, (i) 1 cm, and (ii) 1 μm. The speed of sound in a typical solid is 4000 ms^{-1}.

Chapter 10

1 (a) Verify the derivations of equations (10.4) and (10.5).
(b) (Harder) Find the analogous expression for S for 'intermediate statistics' (see problem 2 for Chapter 5), and check that it has the correct limits.

2 Consider the formation of case 2 vacancies (often called Frenkel defects) as introduced in section 10.3. The defect occurs when an atom leaves a normal site and moves to an interstitial site. Suppose the crystal has N normal sites and N_1 interstitial sites (these numbers will be the same within a small multiple which depends on the crystal structure). The energy of formation of the defect is Φ. Following the method of section 10.3, show that the number n of vacancies at temperature T is

$$n = (NN_1)^{\frac{1}{2}} \exp\left(- \Phi/2k_B T\right).$$

(*Hint*: Disorder now occurs in the arrangement both of the vacancies and of the interstitial atoms.)

Chapter 11

1 Estimate the strength of the effective interaction field (equation (11.2)) in a strong ferromagnet such as iron ($T_C = 1043$ K). You may assume that iron is a spin-$\frac{1}{2}$ solid, with $\mu = \mu_B$. This is not accurate, but it will give an order of magnitude.

2 Estimate the typical ordering temperature for a nuclear spin-$\frac{1}{2}$ solid. Assume that all the nuclei have a moment μ_N, that they are separated by $0.3\,\text{nm}$ and that the interactions arise from the magnetic dipole influence of about eight nearest neighbours. (Don't try to be too accurate!)

3 In the case of beta-brass (section 11.4) show that, in the mean field approximation, the structural contribution to the internal energy may be written as

$$U = U_0 - 2Nm^2V$$

where $U_0 = 2N(V_{\text{CuCu}} + V_{\text{ZnZn}} + 2V_{\text{CuZn}})$, and $V = V_{\text{CuCu}} + V_{\text{ZnZn}} - 2V_{\text{CuZn}}$. Hence derive an expression for the ordering temperature in terms of the bond energy difference V. (*Hint*: Work out the number of each type of bond as a function of the order parameter m, assuming that the occupation of each site is uncorrelated with its neighbours–the mean field assumption.)

Chapter 12

1 Verify that equation (12.4) leads to the FD distribution, as stated in section 12.1.2.

2 (a) If the atoms were interacting with a gas consisting of real (massive) bosons, what equations should replace equation (12.4) in order for the BE distribution to follow? (b) Repeat (a) for a MB gas leading to the MB distribution.

3 Verify that $Z_A = Z^N$, for an assembly of N localized particles, using the multinomial theorem method. (See note 5 after equation (12.7).)

Appendix 6
Answers to questions

Chapter 1

1 $\Omega = 84$; average distribution (1.33, 1.00, 0.71, 0.48, 0.29, 0.15, 0.05, 0, 0...) is almost exponential, as for a large assembly (Chapter 2).

Chapter 3

1 $2.6 \mu B/k_B$.

2 $5.7 \mu K$ to $22 \, mK$; $91 \, kHz$.

4 Note that Z is a perfect square. The limiting value of S is $N k_B \ln 4$.

Chapter 5

1 (a) 9; (1.33, 1.00, 0.78, 0.44, 0.22, 0.11, 0.11, 0, 0, ...)
   (b) 1; (1, 1, 1, 1, 0, 0, 0...).

2 $n_i/g_i = 1/\{\exp[-(\alpha + \beta \varepsilon_i)] - 1\} - (p+1)/\{\exp[-(p+1)(\alpha + \beta \varepsilon_i)] - 1\}$.

Chapter 7

1 1.24 per cent.

2 (a) 2.1 K, (b) 85 K, (c) 43 K, (d) 64 K.

3 (b) 2 (c) pure ortho-deuterium.

4 $x N k_B T$, $y N k_B$.

Chapter 8

1 7.1 eV, 82000 K, $1.7 \times 10^6 \, m s^{-1}$.

2 5.1 K.

4 (a) 139 K, 0.012 eV (c) $\mu/k_B \approx -225$ K.

Chapter 9

2 3.2 K.

4 (a) 3.6 h.

5 $y_{max} = 4.9651\ldots$; max in $u(\nu)$ at $y = 2.8214\ldots$.

6 (c) $20\,\mu K$, $0.2\,K$.

Chapter 11

1 1500 T.

2 About 50 nK.

Index

Adiabatic demagnetization, 38–43
Averaging postulate, 4–5

β and temperature, 22–4, 75
Beta-brass, 152–4
Black-body radiation, 125–8
Boltzmann distribution, 20, 26–7, 31, 160
Boltzmann factor, 27, 140, 152, 158
Bose-Einstein condensation, 115, 117–21
Bose-Einstein gases, 115–31
Bose-Einstein statistics, 73–4, 115–7
Bose temperature, 117
Bosons, 65, 69–70, 115, 124, 155, 159

Classical limit, 49, 70–2, 78–9, 92, 93–5, 108, 120
Clausius-Clapeyron equation, 112–3, 122–3
CMN, 36–45
Cooling methods, 38–43, 113–4
Counting microstates, 10, 11–12, 17–18, 67–72
Counting problems, 166–7
Critical exponents, 151
Curie's law, 45, 149
Curie temperature, 146, 152
Curie-Weiss law, 149, 152

Debye model of lattice vibrations, 129–31
Degeneracy parameter, 78–9, 99–100, 104, 117
Density of states: basic ideas, 52–61; various examples, 101–2, 106, 109, 115, 125–6
Diatomic gases, 87–98
Dispersion relation, 59–60, 129
Distinguishable particles, 16–29, 137–8
Distribution: definition, 6–8; determination of thermal distribution, *see* statistical method; for gases, 62–4
Distribution function, 64, 72–5; *see also* entries under Bose-Einstein, Fermi-Dirac and Maxwell-Boltzmann statistics

Einstein model of vibrations in a solid, 50–1, 129–130
Electrons in metals, 100, 104, 109–10
Energy scales, 48–50, 93
Ensembles, 159–65
Entropy calculations: for FD gas, 108; ferromagnet, 148–9; for isotopes, 132–3; for MB gas, 83–4; for oscillators, 48; for two-state particles, 34–5
Entropy expressions for gases, 134–5

Entropy: statistical definition, 13–15, 24, 28, 83–5, 132, 134
Equipartition of energy, 49, 81, 93–5

Fermi-Dirac gases, 99–114
Fermi-Dirac (FD) statistics, 72–3, 100, 158–9
Fermi energy, 100–5
Fermi surface, 103
Fermions, 65, 68–9, 99
Ferromagnetism, 143–52
Fitting waves into boxes: basis, 53–7; various applications, 77, 101–3, 116, 125, 129
Fluctuations 162–3
Free energy (Helmoltz) F: for assembly at fixed T, 136–7, 161–5; of ferromagnet, 147–8; of localized particles, 28–9; of MB gas, 84–6; of vacancies, 139–40

Gibbs free energy G, 141–2
Gibbs paradox, 86
Grouped distribution, 62–4

Harmonic oscillators, 45–51, 90–1
Heat capacity: of BE gas, 120; of diatomic gas, 89–93; of FD gas, 107; of ferromagnet, 148–9, 151; of hydrogen, 93–8; of MB gas, 82–3; of oscillators, 48; of solids, 128–31; of two-state particles, 33–4
^{3}He liquid, 100, 111–4
^{3}He–^{4}He solutions, 41, 133–4
^{4}He liquid, 115, 121–4
Helium gas, 60–1, 78–9, 111
Hydrogen gas, 93–8

Identical particles, 64–7, 86, 96–8

Internal energy U: of BE gas, 120; of FD gas, 105–7, of MB gas, 82–3; of oscillators, 47–8; of photon gas, 127; of two-state particles, 32–3
Ising model, 144, 164
Isotopic disorder, 132–4

Lagrange undetermined multipliers, 20, 72–3, 137–8
Lambda transition, 122, 151–2
Lasers and negative temperatures, 158
Localized particles, 16–17, 30, 45–6, 134
Long- and short-range order, 144, 151–2, 152–4

Macrostate, 1–3, 135–7, 159–65
Magnetic solids, 35–45, 143–52
Magnetization: of simple solid, 43–5; of conduction electrons, 109–10; of ferromagnet, 143–8
Matter and radiation, 155–8
Maxwell-Boltzmann gases, 76–86, 87–9
Maxwell-Boltzman (MB) statistics, 74, 78–9, 87
Mean field approximation, 144, 153
Metastable states, 133
Microstates, 3–4; and entropy, 13–15
Modified BE distribution, 124–5, 156

Open systems, 165
Order-disorder transformation, 152–4
Order parameter, 142–3, 144, 153
Ortho-para conversion, 97–8

Partition function: definition, 21,

27; factorization in diatomic gas, 88–9; for an assembly, 161–4; of MB gas, 77–8, 82–3; of oscillator, 46–7; of two-state particle, 30–1

Pauli exclusion principle, 66, 100–1, 106, 158

Phase diagram: ^{3}He, 111–2; ^{4}He, 121–4

Phase transitions: classification, 141–3; in BE gas, 119–21; in ferromagnet, 143–52; in ^{3}He, 112–3; in ^{4}He, 121–4; second-order, 141–54

Phonons, 115, 124, 128–31

Photon gas, 115, 124, 125–8, 155–8

Planck radiation formula, 126

Polarization: see spin factor

Pressure P; of BE gas, 120; of FD gas, 107–8; of MB gas, 84–5; of radiation, 128

Rotation in gases, 91–3, 95–8

Sackur-Tetrode equation, 84

Schottky anomaly, 34, 37–8

Second-order phase transitions, 141–3

Speed distribution in gases, 79–82

Spin-1/2 solid, 30–5, 113–4, 143–50

Spin factor: definition, 58–9; various examples, 102, 116, 125, 129

Spontaneous and stimulated emission, 157

Spontaneous magnetization, 143–8

Statistical method: applied to distinguishable particles, 17–20; applied to gases, 62–75; in outline, 8–10; model example, 10–13

Stefan-Boltzmann law, 128

Stirling's approximation, 19, 168–9

Superconducting devices, 40–1

Superfluidity, 41, 122–4

Temperature: statistical definition, 24, 75, 85, 161–2

Thermodynamic properties: calculation methods, 27–9; of BE gas, 120–1; of FD gas, 105–8; of MB gas, 82–6; of oscillators, 46–50; of two-state particles, 32–5

Third law of thermodynamics, 35, 42, 83–4, 133

Transitions between states, 155–9

Translational motion in gases, 87–90

Two-fluid model, 118–21, 123–4

Two-state systems, 30–5

Vacancies in solids, 138–40

Velocity distribution in gases, 79–82

Vibration: in gases, 50, 90–1; in solids, 50–1, 128–31

White dwarf stars, 100, 104

Wien's law, 127